The Hungry Kayaker

David Barnes

Copyright © 2010 by David Barnes
First Edition – August 2010

ISBN
978-1-77067-138-6 (Hardcover)
978-1-77067-160-7 (Paperback)
978-1-77067-099-0 (eBook)

All rights reserved.

No part of this publication may be reproduced in any form, or by any means, electronic or mechanical, including photocopying, recording, or any information browsing, storage, or retrieval system, without permission in writing from the publisher.

Published by:

Suite 300 – 777 Fort Street
Victoria, BC, Canada V8W 1G9
www.friesenpress.com

For information on bulk orders contact:
info@friesenpress.com or fax 1-888-376-7026

Distributed to the trade by The Ingram Book Company

*For Jennifer, my love, my friend,
my tent mate, and my guinea pig.*

Table of Contents:
The Hungry Kayaker

The routines of routine... 1
It's all about the food... 5
Day trippin checklist 7
Ooooops, I need a bandaid 9
Dehydration.. 10
Making a natural poultice.. 12
Burns/cuts/scrapes 13
Blood/eye strain/ mossies 14
Hypothermia... 14
Hyperthermia.. 16
What to wear?... 17
Bad clams!.. 19
A plan, a floaty plan 20
Keeping it clean 21
Setting up your kitchen.. 24
Campfires... 25
Making a fire 26
Kayak sauna... 29
Share and share alike 30

The kayak and the kitchen **33**

Stuffing the hatches... 33
Kayak kitchen checklist.. 36
At home and in camp.. 38
Cooking measurements 40

Breakies **41**

Asparagus Omelet 41
Buckwheat Pancakes 42
Corn Pancakes 43
French toast.. 44
Camp garbage... 45
Go bananas Pancakes... 46

Snacks **47**

Anzac cookies... 47
Bannock 48
Beer fondue... 49

Black bean brownies 50
Chocolate fondue 51
Energy balls. 52
Gorp. 53
Granola bars 54
Hummas pita. 55
Rolling waves chocolate bar 56
Sesame seed cookies 57

Wraps **58**

Chicken, avocado, and bacon 58
Flood tide fajitas. 59
Peanut Butter & banana 60
Tuna wrap. 61

Soup. **62**

Basic backpacker chili 63
Blue jellyfish & celery soup 64
Just plain chicken stew. 65
Chunky pizza soup 66
Leeky kayak potato soup. 67
Mediterranean chicken stew 68
Minty cream of pea soup 69
More rocko stew. 70
Pacific rim beef stew 71
Paddlers soup 72
Spicy sausage stew 73
Super easy chorizo & beans. 74
Veggie chili 75

Pasta **76**

Cheesey beef 76
Cold pasta. 77
Egg noodle with asparagus 78
Orzo in lemon & parmesan cheese .79
Penne with tomato pesto 80

Curry **81**

Chick pea curry 81
Clayoquot curry 82
Curried chicken pita. 83

v

Curried Thai noodles 84
Green chicken curry. 85
Race rocks rice curry 87
Thai shrimp 88
Tidal rapids curry. 89

Stir Fries 90

3 B's stir fry 90
Asparagus mushroom stir fry.. 91
Beef noodles 92
Chicken noodle stir fry.. 94
Chicken, snow peas & cashews 95
Lemon ginger chicken 96
Spicy Thai beef & noodles.. 97
Stir Fried beef & rice 98

Rice.. 99

Creamy asparagus Risotto.. 99
Creamy rice, spinach & chicken 100
Grilled chicken & asparagus Risotto. 101
Hatch cover sushi 102
Pacific rim lentils & rice 103
Zucchini Risotto 104

Campfire grilling. 105

Beef kabobies.. 105
Chicken kabobs in tomato. 107
Lamb kabobies (spicy) 108
Lamb kabobies (tamer). 109
Spicy beef kabobies 110

Assorted dinner ideas 111

Baby seal cakes.. 111
Beer battered oysters 112
Chicken chimichangas 113
Chicken satay over couscous.. 114
Gloop (an old family favorite). 115
Grilled scallops.. 116
Lamb & zucchini 117
Orange ginger Chicken & broccoli 118
Salmon in tomato & orange sauce 119

Sweet and sour lentils .. .. .120
Thai noodle salad 121
Slammin' yammin' quesadillas. .. .. .122

Tea **124**

Chamomile chai 124
Chocolate minty tea. .. .. .125
Cranberry ginger tea 126
London fog. 127
Tookool green tea 128
Vanilla chai 129

At the end of the day. **130**

About the author **133**

the hungry kayaker

preparing for a weekend outing

The Routines of Routine.

Kayaking and camping consist of two things; kayaking, and camping. They are good on their own but in combination make for a great weekend outing. The first thing you will need to go kayak camping is a kayak. Then, all the other stuff that goes with a kayak, and a paddle, a few bits and pieces, and the paddling part is relatively basic. If you think all you need to go kayaking is to pack your boat, sit down, hold onto the paddle and flap your arms around in a rhythmic and hopefully coordinated manner and you will get from A to B, you would be half right. Kayaking is a little more than that. It is a skilled task; it does require some time to develop this specific skill, at least the skills and confidence it takes to go beyond your own backyard waters. Whether an avid experienced kayaker, or novice this book is for you, the weekend paddler whose time is limited.

Let's start with kayaking. I am assuming that if you have picked up this book you are a kayaker and know of what I am speaking in the coming pages. If however, you are not yet a paddler, fear not. It is not very hard to start kayaking, and there are initial start-up costs. I am a poor self-employed writer and I managed in the end to have a yard filled with three kayaks. I was once in the beginning stages of kayaking and launched from a dock by a kayak guide friend of mine one cold autumn evening. This is a handy thing to have if you are just starting out and cannot afford a kayak of your own. For two years, I borrowed kayaks by making myself useful at the kayak dock until the bug for the activity was so embedded I had to break the piggy bank and purchase a boat of my own.

The basic level of kayaking is the novice stage. This is the infant, 'newbie' stage. Most people get to this partly by way of a guided evening tour, including a sunset, chocolate chip cookies and lemonade on a beach provided by the tour operator. You get back home from this and have the kayaking bug. You then head out and buy stuff an overwhelming amount of stuff at the local kayak shop. It is there that you learn the lingo. Rubbing elbows with fit young kayak guides and sun-chiseled tour operators talking about chines, and roto-molded versus fiberglass, and other such terms of the trade. Talk of 'self-rescues', buoyant throw lines, the pros and cons of paddle floats. Kayak jargon such as rocker, rudder and the difference between stern and bow. It is always good to know your back end from your front end.

There is no known cure for this initial stage of the paddling disease, and the symptoms can add up as alarming digits on the credit card bill. As you go along over time that eases up and you fall happily into a rhythm brought about by already having the gear you need. You go kayaking whenever possible. You have taken the safety courses and learned how to perform self-rescues and maybe some clever new paddle techniques. You subscribe to lots of kayaking and paddling magazines, which pile up under your side of the bed. You are now a kayaker and you want to take off with your kayak for the weekend and camp. The idea of simply paddling to some secluded beach and setting up your tent has an attraction that you cannot resist. However, do you know how to camp?

Ah, you see, camping too is a specific skill, and I dare say an art form unto itself more important than just learning to paddle a kayak. Most accidents will occur in or around a camp. Did you know that? In fact, you are much safer on the water. Drowning, yes that is a risk when bobbing about on the sea, I will concede that one, but are you likely to cut yourself or get a nasty burn from your cook stove while paddling? Not likely. Let alone the stubbing of bare toes on all the tripping-falling-down-on-your-face-booby-traps that lay about in campgrounds.

Camping is a skill that some practitioners have taken to extremes. They are the outdoor mercenary types who make the Boy Scouts look like, well, boys. These guys head out on wilderness treks and paddling tours with the bare essentials only. A tarp, a knife and fishing tackle, matches and the crucial skill of savvy inventiveness. They are able to catch, snare, skin and cook just about anything that happens by. They know what plants to eat, and what root and or berry cures any ailment. These guys are adept at the finer points of roughing it. I doubt they bring the fixings for chocolate fondue nights.

Most of us hover around the novice/intermediate levels. Leaving those far advanced outdoorsy types to suffer weeks on end eating nothing but urchins, raw! For they are men, and I, as a foodie and humble paddling bum am content to let them do their thing, and I will do mine. I would say that I flap my paddles at about the level of (my modesty cannot allow more) a confident intermediate, and that goes for my camping skills as well. As for being a foodie, I will never claim to be a professional cook or chef. I have not gone to cooking school however I am a well-practiced maker of meals while camping.

It takes time to develop skills that make the experience of moving about within your camp simple and event-free. For those who only have the opportunity to get out once or twice per year this development may be daunting. We learn from our mistakes and I have made my fair share of them. A few years of sitting in a cold puddle in my kayak seat and I learned how not to splash seawater into my cockpit as I climbed aboard. I learned a few knots, and have developed a routine beginning with loading the kayak, and then to the order in which I set up my camp. Helping me along was a good friend who, in my opinion is the best outdoorsman I know. Watching him, and a few others, I began assimilating some of those methods and adapting them to the way I like to do things. Slowly, but surely I found my way in the outdoors. No longer was I stumbling aimlessly with stubbed toes and wet feet, but able to be warm, dry, and very comfortable with the day to day of camp routines. Not all of you have a buddy with outdoors experience to guide you on your way and to steer you clear of wet bums, bumps and bruises and of course, the oft times folly of cooking in the wilds. This book I hope will be your guide, or at least point you in the right direction.

Routines

Over time I have developed my own camping routines. This word, routine is the base of good easy camping. I know, this is beginning to sound like I am overcomplicating something so enjoyable and seemingly simple as camping out. Bear with me here. Routines are good habits to have out there. Unlike the obsessive routine need to triple-check the front door to convince yourself it is indeed locked, or to look repeatedly to check if you have left the stove on...hang on, that reminds me, I'll be right back!

A good 1,2,3 routine when arriving at your beach camping spot will save you time, some hassles, and perhaps un-necessary discomforts at the end of a long day on the water. In the number one spot, shelters. Packing your tent in the rear hatch so it is easily accessible without pulling out everything and the kitchen sink is a good practice. Keep things of priority handy and that means in the order of need. Your number one priority is a home no matter what the weather may be doing at the time. Pick a tent site that is in the lee of the island or shoreline to keep free of wind. Staying back out of the wind will not compromise your need to see pleasant scenery from your tent door, but will keep your home comfortable. Comfort is camping. Roughing it is what happens when things go awry or for those who claim the need to go 'hard core'. Struggling in a windstorm with rocks holding down the insides of your tent is stressful. Therefore, your nylon abode should be situated shy of the elements. This is not always possible but if you have an idea of which way the winds will be coming from you have half the battle won in placing your tent. I will leave the personal preference of morning light versus evening light to you. I personally like a bright tent in the morning, as I am up early anyway. Consider putting up a tarp over the area beside your tent. I do this so I can get out and dress without wiggling around in a cramped tent or standing in the rain. A tarp set up as a windbreak is a good idea too. My tent is also the last thing I will take down when leaving a camp.

Once your tent is erected, it is time to start hauling up all the bits and pieces as you launch into part two of your new routine. Keep and eye on your kayak while pitching your tent and bringing up the gear. Repeat after me, 'Trust in Ala, but tie up your camel!' Your kayak is all you have. As with your tent, your kayak is home when out on a tour. It carries all you need, food, water, and shelter. Lose it to the incoming tide or a random wave from a passing boat's wake and you are snookered. Pull up your boat, as heavy as it may be above the tide line and if you have landed on an incoming tide, you will have to repeat this. Placing some kelp in front of your heavy kayak will make it easier to pull up, as well as when it is time to launch. Remember to tie your boat onto something. I try to get unloaded quickly. It gets the circulation going again and keeps you warm. On cooler days I will keep wearing my PFD (personal floatation device) while I am setting up camp. It acts well as an insulator and keeps my torso warm. When the boat is empty, it is a priority to get the kayak out of harms way up on logs well above the storm tide line and of course, once again, tie up your camel. A good indicator of the highest tidemark is the line of flotsam and dried seaweed. Any place above that should be fine. Do double-check a tide table just in case. Unpack what you need, as you need it. I like to get my kitchen up and running first so I can put on a brew while changing into my camp clothing. Camping does take a certain amount of multi-tasking, i.e. boiling water on your stove as you change into your sweater.

Now we arrive at stage three, camp time. This is when everything slows down. It is time to relax and enjoy the sense of achievement that comes with getting there under your own steam. Contained in a separate dry bag left unopened in the tent is the clothing that will 'only be worn in camp'. I cannot stress enough the need to keep a change of dry warm clothing. I carry two sets. One set of clothing I wear while kayaking. Yes, this clothing will get a tad stinky and wet. Never paddle in your 'camp clothes'. If for some reason you do this, you will end up with nothing but wet clothing and this will cut your trip short. Your camp clothing bag should be treated in the same way as your sleeping bag. When unloading your kayak this bag goes directly into the tent, and kept dry. I should mention that packing and unpacking your sleeping bag should be done in the confines of your tent to keep it from getting wet on rainy days. In my camp clothing bag I keep dry socks (rarely worn, but well-traveled companions) a long sleeve shirt, t-shirts, shorts, a spare pare of quick-dry pants and a wind breaker. For evening wear, I bring fleece wear. Polar fleece pants, a fleece jacket, and even a toque. The sensation of refreshment after slipping out of your paddling clothes and into your camping clothing cannot be understated. Heavenly, and of course I would add a freshly brewed americano to enjoy before leaping into making dinner.! Now it is time to eat.

It's all about the food

Why good food, the answer is, why not? When I first fell off the sofa many eons ago in an avalanche of potato chip crumbs, salt and vinegar I seem to recall, it was to follow an old high school friend up a mountain. Who knows why I went from seasoned couch potato to high altitude adventurer over-night. One day, I guess the spring snapped on my sofa and off I went onto the floor, from there it was only an upward climb. I invited myself along on a one-day outing with little or no clue, or preparation, nor appropriate footwear. I had runners on my feet not hiking boots. Oh, how I suffered the days after that momentous hike in which I failed to reach the summit. My body rebelled and seized up to the point that crawling was my best option. I lounged on a craggy ledge with my friend's soon-to-be wife who endured my endless babbling about the meaning of life. I found myself having a mid-mountain epiphany instead of a mid-life crisis! She insisted I drink some water, and to eat my noodles, and shut up. She did not actually tell me to shut up, but if she was not thinking it at the time, she is up for sainthood.

The epiphany was part dehydration, part exertion and lack of carbohydrates, and part rubber mallet to the metaphoric noggin. I was still going on and on after my noodles but not as fast. The noodles were good, freeze-dried fair that sustained me on future mountainside lunch breaks during my brief pre-kayaking stint as a hill wanderer. I soon tired of lugging all my belongings up mountains on my back and found kayaking much more to my liking, and I could float the gear instead of carrying it. This is good!

I paddled for years bringing along what I called, lazy guy meals. Boil in a bag, freeze-dried tasteless meals that had sufficient nutrient in them to keep me alive, but what is the point of living if there is not one mouthful of good flavourful satisfaction involved? Some time went by and low and behold, I had a new kayaking mate joining in on trips to the coast. With him came a bag of spices, seasonings, meats, veggies, sauces galore. He mocked my bubbling plain brown bag of goop flopped pathetically in a cook pot of boiling water. I stood, headlamp illuminating my steaming stove and had no reply in defense of my meal choices. How could I defend myself while squeezing out snotty substances over minute rice, while he was performing culinary camp alchemy with pinches of this and that? I had to change my ways.

I concluded that there was no good reason for not eating as well in camp as I could, and did at home. For many years, I had lived alone and enjoyed cooking for myself. I had gathered a number of good, easy to make and more importantly, fast to make 'single guy' dinners. They amounted to basic bachelor cooking, gourmet style at times and there was no reason I could not make them while out camping. Most of them could be whipped up simply using one pot as well, which comes in handy when using a single burner camp stove that fits in the kayak's hatch. With some trial and error and the occasional scrubbing out burned rice at the seashore, I narrowed them down to the favorite recipes that appear in this book. I leave some room for your own trial and error and experimentation, as cooking in general, and especially cooking outdoors require the chef to be flexible.

Kayaking is a work and reward sport. You work your body paddling all day, sometimes to utter exhaustion and are rewarded with a wilderness beach and a private showing of the best sunset ever. So then, why scarf down a bowl of Ramen noodles when you can have homemade Moroccan stew. With some forethought and preparation at home, that benefited me while cooking in camp; I discovered an entirely new aspect of outdoor living. The sunset looks a whole lot better with a steaming bowl of Moroccan stew in your hands.

The weekend paddler

Many of my kayaking trips have put my beloved wooden kayak, Dragonfly, and I into tall bouncy rolling swells that come to crashing deaths on rocky rugged shores. My view was constantly changing from cliffs and green tree covered mountains, to seemingly endless ocean horizons with nothing lying between my bow and Japan but a lot of H2O. Many more trips have been spent paddling in my backyard waters of the Southern Gulf Islands. It is these shorter jaunts of a day or two days that I do the most, and I am not alone. Landing on any of the islands included in the B.C. Marine Trail network, I meet others like myself. People enjoying nature and enjoying the kayaking experience in short weekend snapshots.

Not everyone can book off ten to fourteen days or even longer to go paddling. This leaves a more realistic time between Fridays and Sundays to pull out the camping gear, kayak, paddles and goodies to sneak off and mess about with boats. Anyone who has read the Wind and the Willows will know what I mean.

To that end, I hope in these pages I can relate some of my trade secrets (unwilling as I am to give away my marinade recipe for spicy beef) and nudge you in the ways of good, enjoyable, ethical no-trace camping, and some tasty meal ideas too!

> Tip:
> Pre-chop, peel, or measure your ingredients ahead of time and pack in Ziploc bags. Remembering to label them to avoid mystery meals.

Day Trippin' Checklist.

Yes, sadly it is true that most accidents happen at home, or close to home. You can slip in the shower, fall off a ladder while changing a light bulb, and we just won't go into messiness about mishaps with power tools. The same can be said for kayaking. More often than not we are paddling close to home in our own backyard waters. Living in the Gulf Islands as I do, this is a common theme. It is easy to become complacent in these cozy calm local waters. Day paddling gives a false conclusion that 'nothing can happen, because I am close to home'.

Day or even weekend paddling should be taken as seriously in the planning stages as you might for a multi-day excursion to the wilds. Heading onto the water at anytime comes with possible unexpected events. A case in point was a friend's simple canoe paddle across the Trincomali Channel between Salt Spring and Galiano Island. A short afternoon paddle to look at the eroded sand stone cliffs of Galiano Island ended in a minor epic of sorts in high wind waves, and an uncomfortable night sleeping on a found wooden pallet barely above the tide line.

Often mistakes made on the water has lead me to some of nature's little treats such as paddling into a raft of Blue Sail Jellies in Barkley Sound because we took a wrong turn around the wrong island. Then there was the time I was privileged to a pod of orca swimming past due to taking five minutes longer on a break after crossing Johnstone Strait. Sometimes however, it can be a little more serious. The key items you will need on any multi-day tour are the same things that will make even the most unexpected of events on a day paddle palatable. The key ingredients are having enough drinking water, food, and the means to stay dry and warm. The Boy Scouts had it right, "be prepared".

My rule of thumb is that on any day trip I assume I might become stuck some place and possibly have to spend the night. I am not going to suggest that you bring along the entire camping regalia every time you want to go for a quickie, but consider this.

It is a beautiful summer day. The sun is shining, not a cloud in the sky, and a light breeze rippling the water from the Northwest. This could not be better paddling conditions right? After an hour or so, you come across your favorite spot. A small crushed shell beach, a grassy meadow above it shaded by tall gangly Arbutus and long-branched Fir trees. You decide to stop for a lunch break here among the wildflowers. From your kayak's hatch, you pull out your lunch pack and beside it, your maybe you have packed a tent or even a tarp. Why bring them? Because in about half and hour you will come to the conclusion that it is far too hot to keep paddling further. Instead staying right where you are for the afternoon, and take a nap. You erect your tent, or string up the tarp to keep the wind and sun off you while you snooze, and a good thing that you brought a book along. I have done this, I guarantee the calming affects of kayak napping afternoons.

An alternative ending to this happy tale is the reality of Mother Nature being a bit fickle at times. Your sunny day becomes dour and cloudy in less than half and hour after you began paddling. The summer winds turn more autumn-like and strong. Whipping up increasingly bigger seas and horizontally aligned rainfall. You paddle madly to the first available landing and bail-out. Thankfully, you brought along that tarp or tent, and extra food, oh and of course, a book to read to pass the time as you may be there a while. It is of course a good idea to check the forecast beforehand, but with so many of my day paddles, the forecast was not as advertised.

Here are some ideas as to what to carry in your kayak on a day trip. These may not be enough to sustain you on a longer journey, but are the basics. The most important item to bring is knowledge. Be sure to have up-to-date weather and tide forecasts. I have seen things change in very short order out there, even on a quiet afternoon. Wind is the kayaker's nemesis and only you can be the judge of how much work you want on a paddle day. Carry a VHF radio, or at the very least a cell phone. The outdoor manufacturers are wise to the gadget dependent, and have come up with a colourful array of watertight bags, and cases. Get a heads up on tides and which way they are going during your planned time of paddling. Arranging your kayaking travels to allow the tidal currents to push you along is far nicer than paddling up stream against the tide. Knowing this also give you a head start on what type of wave action you may encounter. A wind coming from the opposite direction of the tide is like brushing the hair backwards on the cat, with similar results. A tide running in the same direction of the winds will cause ripples and maybe a light chop. Crosswinds to the tidal direction are, playful. Before you head out, let someone know that you are going paddling and where, and try not to paddle alone if possible.

A kayak is a good thing to bring on a paddling day, but make sure that your hatches are secure, and watertight. Make sure you have a buoyant paddle, a spare under the deck bungees and a non-leaking spray skirt. I once saw someone paddling with a garbage bag around his waist as a spray skirt. It will do in a pinch if for some chance reason you lost yours somewhere during the trip. He had not, this was what he was using, do not do this! The skirt has a purpose other than making you look silly on dry land. It keeps the water from getting in, especially when capsized. Your cockpit is an air pocket, kayakers like air pockets, especially, when they find themselves upside-down!

On your PFD (personal floatation device) carry a good knife that is easily accessible. Wear your PFD! Many kayaks are found without a paddler in them and the life jacket tucked neatly under the deck lines. My knife is in a holder pointed vertically so that I can get at it with either hand immediately, and the handle does not get in the way of my movements. You should also have a whistle and a beacon light if possible. Hang your headlamp from a carabineer or purchase a deck light that can also hang on a lanyard that can be hooked onto your PFD. It is a good idea to have a deck light on your kayak even if you don't think you will be paddling after dark. Most boaters cannot see you on radar. Kayakers are called speed bumps for a reason. Be seen, don't be a bump. A little trick is to put an empty wine bag found inside any boxed wine on your decking. They are metalic and should show up on radar.

I carry a small 5 litre dry bag, and this is secured into the cockpit on a leash. Should I flip over the contents of that bag are my essentials and tying it in is just a good idea not to lose them. In that bag I carry a small first aid kit, a roll of duct tape as a kayak band-aid kit, flares and a flare gun, my VHF radio, sunscreen, lip balm (SPF rated), sunglasses, snacks, point an shoot digital camera, and binoculars. If there is room, I will toss in extra camera batteries that also work in my lights and anything else but the kitchen sink is shoved into that bag. For camping I have a watertight kit box full of goodies, but for a day paddle that usually does not come for the ride. Bring a good lunch and the items you will need to prepare it should you require a bit of cooking. Dress for the conditions and maybe bring a small dry bag with some extra clothing in it. A fleece jacket is an amazing thing! Wear a hat and sunglasses and bring the rain gear just in case.

All this stuff may sound a bit extreme and bordering on over-kill. Nevertheless, when you spend a night huddled shivering on a wobbling wooden pallet on the edge of a sand stone cliff, wishing you had never left the safety of your sofa, you will thank me.

Oooops, I Need a Band-Aid!

Things just happen don't they. Going out for a day of kayaking sounds benign enough, the weather forecast is mild and fair. The sun is shining and the seas are calm. However, we can never really forecast the unexpected mishaps that are inherent with outdoor pursuits. No matter what you are doing, whether it a day out on the water, or a multi-day expedition, you really should carry a first aid kit. It is not good enough to simply carry one either, it helps if you have some idea of how to use it, and the contents therein. There are a few good basic manuals for wilderness first aid on the market. Many of the scarier items in the first aid books such as altitude sickness and cerebral edema can be glanced over for entertainment value, but hardly relate to kayaking and camping. Altitude sickness for instance is at sea level is highly unlikely, but receiving sunburn is likely. What should you do for that intense headache? What should you do for that minor burn you received from the cook stove?

Most accidents will occur near or in your campsite. You are safer on the water with the zooming speedboats and wind waves than you are on land. With outdoor cooking, there is the added factor of working with open flame in less than idea conditions, i.e. your stove tipping over thus spilling hot contents down your shins and onto your bare feet. Hot metal objects and sharp utensils tossed in the mix and all used while whipping up a gourmet meal by the glow of headlamp light after the sun has gone down.

The three most common accidents when cooking on a beach log are burns, scolding, and carnage from the previously mentioned sharp objects. Sadly, you can add the entire pot of dinner falling off the log into the sand and rendered inedible...yes, this has happened to me, and those I love. This section will cover those and a few other ailments and discomforts acquired in pursuing an outdoor life. In this section, I am offering a few natural methods of handling these episodes, but by no means do I suggest that ground sage leaves and juniper berries can replace a standard medical kit accompanied with a manual for quick reference and a general knowledge of first aid. Here I will go back to some basics. Good, old wives solutions and remedies. Or, is it more correct these days to say something along the lines of, Advanced Age Spousal Counseling? At any rate, when you find yourself at the end of a long paddling day, blistered and aching it can be tough to muddle through and enjoy your surroundings to the fullest. More often than not, it is one of the most basic of needs that has not been met causing you the most discomfort. The immediate remedy for most complaints from headaches to fatigue is simple H2O.

Dehydration and the most natural cure.

If it aches, if it is stiffening up, or if feeling at all fatigued, then just add water. The leading contributor to most ailments resulting from outdoor activities comes from not drinking enough water. A common excuse I hear for not hydrating enough is, 'if I drink lots of water then I will have to pee a lot'. Yes, there is an unquestionable cause and affect going on here. The reality is that a well-hydrated paddler's bladder will not likely feel the urge to stop for a break along the way. Unlike drinking too much coffee, or even tea the body uses every drop of pure water you give it to nourish cells and keep everything in your body lubricated, and running smoothly. Water is not a diuretic but can be known to carry bugs that will cause this affect. Overall, clean fresh water is less likely to cause you to require the ironic need to stop and rummage for your empty water bottle so you can urinate into it while out on the sea. Or, quickly locating the most popularly named places on our trips. Places named, 'Take a leak cove...Take a leak bay, Take a leak inlet, Take a leak island', and so on. This happens more from drinking copious mugs of coffee before setting out.

Dehydration is sneaky. Unlike its aggressive cousin hypothermia, becoming dehydrated is something that sneaks up on the paddler. You can be dehydrated and not really be aware of it until the body has had enough and begins to scream for a drink. The first thing that happens is that the nervous system goes wonky. Nerves contract from lack of hydrated cells and the first indication of dehydration will be a throbbing headache. Lesser exertion and the lesser the headache, but it is an indicator that something is definitely wrong. Fatigue usually follows and by now, it will take more time to recover. The body can go for some great length of time without nourishments, but lasts only days without adequate water. Stay dehydrated for a long time and you will die a rather excruciating death.

Even the minor affects of dehydration will put a considerable damper on you enjoyment. You will end up lying in your tent popping ibuprofen tablets while your hydrated friends are out having fun. My advice is to put the pills away and fill up your water bottle. Lie in your tent and slowly, I repeat slowly drink litre upon litre, you will not want another drop, but keep drinking. The aching will go away, and your liver will respect you in the morning for not making it deal with the drugs. I have always struggled with getting enough to drink. The water bottle became a problem issue in the kayak. It was either out of reach under the deck and spray skirt so on wavy days access was a problem. Or it was under the deck bungees and no longer cold and refreshing, but heated by the sunshine and far less attracting as a beverage.

I had to stop thinking of water as simply that, a beverage, but a part of the kayak experience and necessary to keep going. Having your water bottle under the deck or strapped onto the deck can create accessibility issues. Then there is the problem of fiddling with bottles and loose lids! This had to stop. I found a way to solve the temperature dilemma of having a water bottle on the deck in the sun as well as accessibility. I went to the outfitters and purchased a heavy-duty dromedary bag. This is a water bag made of durable material, it held over ten litres of water and could take a pounding. It fit perfectly in that little used space behind my seat and I ran an attached drinking tube through a hole I drilled in my deck and the mouthpiece snaps into a clip. Instant no fuss hydration at a moments notice, and I could even suck on my tube while still paddling.

How much water should you bring? Good question, I'm glad you asked! A good average is about four litres per person, per day. About a litre of which will be allocated to cooking, the rest you should drink. Make sure that it is clean and fresh and your containers are the same. The above-mentioned dromedary bags come in all sizes and fit nicely into the hatches. I have two, one behind my seat and the other wedged flat up against the front bulkhead in the forward hatch. It makes for good ballast as well so try not to store your water supply at the far back or front of the kayak. I pack heaviest to lightest from the cockpit out.

Water can carry unwanted friends. If you are running low on fresh water and find a stream or creek on your travels, go ahead fill your bags but be careful. Giardaisis, a.k.a. Beaver Fever comes down stream from the upper watersheds and flows through the not-so-sanitary practices of local animals. Giardia lamblia is of the protozoan family. It is transmitted through the excrement of both animals and humans and if ingested will affect you in a couple of stages. Again, just like dehydration problems, Giardia is sneaky, and will only present symptoms after 7 – 10 days and can be confused with the flu. It comes with chronic diarrhea, bloating, fatigue, and for added fun, abdominal cramping resulting in weight loss. It can be treated effectively with prescription drugs, but why get to that fun place of chronic anything by careful and treating all 'found water'.

There are many ways to do this. Boiling the water is the most basic of solutions. Bringing your water to a good five-minute rolling boil should kill off unfriendly bugs. The drawback of this method on any outing is the requirement of heavy use of camp fuel in performing a long boiling session, and the water can end up tasting rather flat.

Treating water with chemicals is another solution. A bag of iodine tablets or crystals is easy to carry. A small fact to remember about iodine is toxicity. Ingesting crystallized iodine is very dangerous and people with thyroid issues should avoid using the iodine methods of purifying drinking water. Iodine tablets and crystals are effective in combating Giardia, but results vary with water temperatures and contact times. As a last resort, I would go with iodine, but I prefer filtration. I carry a small hand-pump filter that is readily available from most outdoor stores for about the $100 range. They come with a removable ceramic filter that is reusable, easy to clean and very reliable for screening out the microbes. The pump is equipped with a hose, which lays in the puddle, pond, or stream, and as you pump (at the rate of approximately one litre per minute), clean water is deposited right into your dromedary bag or Nalgene bottles. Try to pump drinking water from moving water rather than standing water if possible.

Making a natural poultice.

This is a treatment method that has been sent packing by over the counter packaged medical treatments, but the old ways should not be ignored, as they are indeed tried and true ways. These poultices will do the job if you are stuck and have your Hungry Kayaker kitchen bag well stocked. Some of this may sound like the recipes I have included in this book. No, you are not adding one more recipe to the 101 ways to serve man, but you can relieve a few ailments with a little wheat germ. I remember my mother concocting a small poultice of wheat germ for bee stings. Another good way to ease the pain of a sting is to dab some good black mud on the area. Unlike a store-bought cure such as Afterbite mud actually draws out the stinger and toxins. To make a poultice use your dried herbs rubbed in your hand. If the dried herbs are not too powdery, they are the best to use. Place them in a cup and add just enough cold water to make a paste that is not too runny. It has to stay in place on the affected area. Mix it well and apply, then covering with a dressing. The important thing is to try to keep as much of the moisture of the poultice in against the affected area as much as possible.

Starting with the first problem, most paddlers have when getting into the sport, that being soreness of muscles and blisters. Blisters on the hands are due to one little kayaking mistake. To avoid blisters you must train your hands to relax, but at the same time remain in control of the paddle shaft. Blisters occur because of holding on to the paddle too tightly, both on the forward and on the drawing strokes. The first thing I tell a new paddler is to hold the shaft lower to the deck. Raising hands too high cause end of the day soreness and the following day will not be fun either. Lowering your hands to chest level or below will not only decrease the risk of aching muscles but will increase the power of your paddle stroke. The longer the blade is in the water, the more water it draws. Dipping your kayak paddle down deep lifts your arms higher and can in some cases act as a lever pulling you over. Remember, you are paddling a kayak, not a canoe. A good easy paddle stroke will ease having those sore muscles later on. The blisters as I mentioned, happen due to rubbing + friction = blisters.

Of course, had you read this section before you went out paddling willy-nilly you would not be bothered with nasty blisters on your hands. Okay, I'll help you out then. The first thing not to do with blisters is to open them. I know that it lays there all bulbous, fluid-filled and tempting. Just a little squeeze, come on, you know you want to. Don't! If a blister should burst open then immediately wash it with soap and water, let the affected area dry. Apply vitamin E cream and cover with a band-aid. Making a poultice of wheat germ, or even olive oil if that is all you have on hand. Applying more cream and fresh band-aids until healed. Avoiding more paddling for a time. This will do you a world of good until it has healed. However, should you need to get back on the water right away, wear a pair of cycling gloves for paddling. You'll look cool with them on and they will reduce the rubbing on your open wounds.

Burns, even minor burns are in actuality an open wound and should be treated as seriously. Any broken areas on the skin are open to invading infections and in this case do NOT apply salves or lotions. Clean the area carefully and pat dry. Extreme care must be made in dressing this area with sterile bandages or gauze. Seek medical treatment as soon as possible with any burns. In the case of minor scalds or burns immediately, immerse the burned area in cold water for 5 minutes or more. Do not pour water over the wound as this will not aid in the cooling of the skin. Burning is just that, cooking your flesh and as with any other meat (yes we are made of meat) it will continue to burn even after it is removed from direct heat. The cold water will cool the flesh. Remove from cold water and carefully remove any dirt with a saltwater solution (1 teaspoon salt to 1 cup cold water) by pouring this very gently over the burn and never touch the burned area directly. Carefully dry the area, not by rubbing but with gentle patting and air dry. Apply a cool natural poultice to the area made of wheat germ but it is my feeling in the situations involving burns to avoid applying anything. Keep the wound clean, dry and covered with a cloth dressing. Keep covered for three days before changing the dressing, and get to a doctor as soon as possible.

Cuts and scrapes are the most likely of any thing to happen in camp. I come home from camping trips with mystery wounds that I do not remember inflicting upon myself. They are usually small. Should you cut yourself, wash the cut well with a saltwater solution. Lightly apply a wheat germ poultice or vitamin E cream. Brew up a tea poultice of chamomile, or comfrey. Bathe the area with the tea, cold tea that is, or cover with a body temperature poultice. Cover with a band-aid or dressing.

Blood. If you cut me, do I not bleed? Yeppers! For minor cuts wash the area well with a saltwater solution, and yes, this will sting. What will sting more is the sprinkle of cayenne you will now apply. This will help stop the bleeding. A comfrey poultice applied to the area and covered with a clean cloth dressing. If there is excessive bleeding then seek medical assistance as soon as possible. To treat bruises make a warm poultice of comfrey or cayenne applying it directly to the wound, let it set for about 5 minutes. Remove and apply a fresh poultice and cover with a dressing. Leave it on overnight.

Eye Strain
Well that was dumb, you forgot your sunglasses now have to put tea in your eyes. Make a chamomile tea. Soak a cloth in the tea and let it become cold. Lay the wet cloth over your closed eyes and if a little tea gets in your eyes, that is alright. Do this with a freshly tea soaked cloth a few times for about 5 minutes each. You should feel less effected by the sun's glare at the end of the day.

Mossies! For some reason mosquitoes don't enjoy me. I get one or two bites while companions are eaten alive all evening long. However, there is a way to lessen the blood loss. Taking vitamin B complex each day will help. Rubbing on eucalyptus oils too, or if you are looking for a quick fix there are loads of repellents on the market. This little mixture will aid in repelling them as well. 1 part citronella, 1 part camphor and ½ part oil of cedar; mixed with olive oil. Lemon juice or vinegar on the bites if all else fails.

Too cold, Too hot

Hypothermia. Hypothermia and Hyperthermia are the two most likely ailments you will encounter when in the outdoors, and are not circumstances reserved for the extreme sports crowd alone. These afflictions have no boundaries, and will sneak when kayaking, camping, or any task that has you exposed to the elements.

Hypothermia means that the person is cold right down to the bone and the body can no longer defend itself. The warmer blood rushes away from the extremities to the vital organs. Arms, legs, hands, feet, fingers and toes are all expendable according to the body's needs. Hypothermia comes in stages and if the person affected becomes colder, they will die. Prevention is best, but if things go downhill, Hypothermia can be caught in its early stages. Immersion in cold west coast waters is the best way to contract Hypothermia. The water here is cold! You can become Hypothermic even in camp especially on windy, wet days. No matter the time of year, or the type of person, Hypothermia can set in and hits its victims very rapidly. The first symptom is severe shivering, chattering teeth and chills. Most people get to this stage of Hypothermia at some point in a lifetime. An example of this are the foolish few, who on January 1 polar bear swims hit the teeth chattering stage while wrapped in blankets as they sip hot chocolate.

As the body heat diminishes the next evidence of hypothermia is the extremities, fingers and lips will turn bluish in colour. The next stage after this is confusion and poor judgment setting in. The indicator that temperature levels in the body are reaching a danger point is when the shivering becomes sporadic in nature. Confusion becomes irrational behaviour as the brain functions slow down. Respiration slows as well and this increases the loss of body heat. Unconsciousness can be next. At this point, the person is in grave danger. Stage three, can result in cardiac arrest. Please note that once you begin CPR you must continue until emergency medical rescue arrives. Also, keep in mind a person suffering Hypothermia is not considered dead until they are pronounced warm and dead. A sobering thought, but I drum this one in harder, as it is a real factor in paddling, mountaineering or any back country activity, and I do count sea kayaking as a back country sport. You may be well away from immediate hospital or ambulance assistance while out paddling.

Treatment of stage one is relatively simple. Warm the person up, but slowly. Hot drinks while they are wrapped blankets or in a warm and dry sleeping bag. Sit them by a campfire once you feel it is safe to leave them long enough to build a good fire. There is a running debate in the wilderness first aid community about the use of direct body heat to warm up a Hypothermic person. The theory is that skin-to-skin transfer of heat from one to the other will work and has been the practice for years. Now it is thought that the person giving aid in this manner may become cold as well and both persons ending with below average body temperatures.

A hot drink of tea with honey, and more of it will do the trick as well for the initial stage of Hypothermia. Remember they (the victims) are not considered goners until proclaimed as such by a professional medical technician and some more severely Hypothermic people have been successfully revived. Professionals must treat someone suffering severe Hypothermia (that is stage two or three), and any treatment that is too aggressive at any stage can cause harm.

- Do your best to prevent Hypothermia in the first place by wearing clothing suitable for immersion, and keep a dry bag in the kayak with clean dry and warm clothing, just in case. Wear a hat always as your head leaks heat the most. Layering is key to keeping body warmth in not out. Layering traps air and keeps you warm. Polypropylene under layers topped with fleece and a water/windproof garments as an outer layer. If you are out on a cold day and stop to take a break, find shelter out of the wind and stay in your paddling vest. It will keep your torso warm. If you are not already in rain pants, slip a pair on whenever you are out of the kayak. Dress for paddling long before you head out on the water so your core temperature is already up. Once your camp is set up, change into your warm dry camp clothing. It feels good to whip on a sweater at the end of a paddling day anyway, and you might just save your own life by doing so.

Hyperthermia

By now, you are wondering if you ever want to leave the sofa again. There was some safety under the chip crumbs, fear not. As nasty as it all sounds I continue now with the next scary item on the list of things to beware Hypothermia's alter-ego, Hyperthermia. Hyperthermia is what happens when we get overheated. It also can lead to your demise, but most people who suffer hyperthermia will only experience nausea of varying severity. The prevention is simple and goes right back to the beginning of simply drinking enough water. Any cold fluids will stave off the onset of Hyperthermia. Yes, even a cold beer will do, but I don't think it qualifies as a remedy. Beer, cold and tasty is not good for you and can lead to dehydration.

Okay, so I sounded a bit like a boring fuddy-duddy there. I will try not to ruin things too much more. Another way of preventing Hyperthermia is to avoid sunburn. I know this is tough. It falls under the category of the age-old kayaker dilemma of wanting a nice hot sunny summer day to go for a paddle, and wishing the sun was not so much an enemy. Paddling on the west coast of British Columbia is a good way to avoid those sunny days. It is called the 'wet coast' for good reason. I digress.

Hyperthermia comes with nausea, headache, cramping, general fatigue, hyperventilation, dizziness and as you might guess, thirsts as well. Like Hypothermia, becoming overheated to such extremes is very dangerous and can be life threatening. As with Hypothermia, treatment should be a slow, non-aggressive procedure. In this case, you don't want to warm the patient. They are already too warm. To treat Hyperthermia, first get out of the direct sun and find a shaded area as soon as possible, and then apply cold cloths to the neck, armpits, scalp and groin. Drink slowly and repeatedly in small sips to avoid shocking the system. Have some salty snacks on hand too. These will replenish your electrolytes. Now climb into a nice shady hole (your tent will do) and get lots of rest.

Preventing the onset of any of the hypo/hyper's is the best bet and easy enough to do. In the case of cold weather paddling, dress accordingly, same goes for hot weather paddling. I avoid the heat of mid-day sun by paddling in the early morning hours. This also bestows some amazing morning lighting upon me for photography. Morning hours are generally calmer on the water as the heating during the day will cause winds to build. By noon, I am usually in camp napping in the shade. Drink water. I cannot drive that one home hard enough can I? Get wet too. If you take a break on a hot paddling day, go for a dip. As the day progresses, keep some salted snacks in your cockpit bag. Take a pee now and then. If your urine is dark that is a true signal you are becoming dehydrated. Apply sunscreen liberally onto dry skin it lasts longer that way. SPF 30 or higher. Wear a good broad-rimmed hat, and soak it in the sea now and then. Sunglasses too, and drink more water!

Okay, I think that about covers the first aid basics. Just remember it is all good fun, but you are on an ocean that is a living creature in its own way. You pat the bum of a horse when you walk behind one. You let a dog sniff your hand before petting one. You dress accordingly, drink lots of water and with luck, you will not open your first aid kit at all and save your juniper berries and wheat germ to make pancakes in the morning when heading out for a paddling day.

What to wear?

Clothing is just as important as the food you will eat, and the tent that you will sleep in. Good choices in outdoor wear will keep your body warm in cold wet conditions and in warm weather will aid in cooling you while out on the water, and later in camp. Dressing for the wet marine environment starts with an understanding of what each fabric does. Layering of these garments will make your travels in the outdoors easier and you can avoid much the above-mentioned hypo/hyperthermic conditions by properly regulating your core body temperature. Most outdoor clothing is made from synthetic materials, but natural fabrics can be useful in the right conditions. All these fabrics are made by inter-weaving fibres to create air pockets. These are dead air spaces providing insulation. However, this insulation is only effective if the fabric also has the ability to breath to avoid the dangers of over-heating. Layering of garments of different thicknesses and moisture wicking properties is the key ingredient. To give you a bit of an idea of what you will be confronted by in clothes shopping for your weekend outing I have listed below various materials. All are used in outdoor gear and the wise combination of these makes for good layering.

Wool – Wool is a good outdoor fabric choice as working as your outer layer. It provides excellent insulation, especially if it gets wet. The drawback of wearing wool is that it becomes incredibly heavy if soaking wet.

Down - Down is an amazing natural insulator, a million ducks and geese cannot be wrong. The drawback of wearing a wet down garment is that it loses all its insulating values because the feathers clump up together and close the dead air pockets. Best save this natural fibre for dryer conditions.

Cotton – Cotton should be avoided as a paddling garment. It has earned the nickname of 'death cloth' for good reason. We all wear cotton t-shirts all summer long. They are comfortable but when wet they do not dry easily and can absorb many times its weight in moisture. Wearing wet cotton will result in your core temperature dropping due to conduction, which means any contact with wet clothing will pull all the heat away from your body.

Synthetic fabrics will be primarily what you will be wearing on a kayaking trip.

Polyester and Polypropylene – These are common in the outdoor clothing market as a great wicking layer. Meaning the material both holds heat to the body as well as possessing excellent breath ability. This fabric dries very quickly and when wet retains a high insulating value. A polypropylene shirt is a good choice for a sunny day, but will not work well against windy conditions. It is at these times that the layering kicks in with a shell of polar fleece for more insulation.

Neoprene – This material is made from closed-cell foam and used in wet suits, paddling gloves and booties. It is available in various thicknesses and which thickness you choose is up to you, and the conditions you will plan to paddle.

Nylon – Nylon is a material commonly used in rain and wind gear. Nylon is not waterproof on its own and must be treated to be fully insulating. These garments are coated by the manufacturer with a breathable laminated coating. Gore-Tex is an example of this. A good nylon layer is the cap on the top of a layering routine.

It requires a bit of experimentation on layering practices. Orchestras of clothing combinations involving the above list of fabrics will help regulate your body temperature while paddling both on and off the water. Layering first with a thin polypropylene/polyester shirt to wick away moisture while retaining warmth. Over that a second layer of polypropylene/polyester in the form of a long-sleeved shirt or a fleece jacket, then a wind/water proof shell over that. Remember your head is a prime source of heat loss. Wear a hat. Paddling pants made of synthetic material as well. In warmer conditions, a polypropylene layer may be all you require.

By adding and removing layers during the day and in the evening as well you can regulate your core body temperature easily. In camp, this is also a concern as hypothermia can sneak in. Remembering that your campsite is as much part of the marine environment as the ocean you had paddled.

> Tips:
> A portion of the water you drink has been drunk by someone else, maybe several times over.

Bad Clams!

PSP's and HAB's are not LOL

Paralytic Shellfish Poisoning, or P.S.P. also known as red tide is no laughing matter. P.S.P.'s and H.A.B.'s, Harmful Algal Blooms are naturally occurring in the environment. The murky reddish-brown discolouration of the water during the warmer summer months is nothing more than a growth of algae. I have seen it occur as early as April or May and as late as October. The poison causing shellfish harvesting closures is a naturally occurring toxin produced by the phytoplankton responsible for the bloom. This toxin builds up in the fleshy meat of the shellfish that we so enjoy in mussels, snails, clam, and oysters. Even barnacles can be contaminated with this as they too feed on phytoplankton that drifts by their stationary homes.

The theory of it being safer to harvest these species in certain months has been proven false, as many species can remain infected with the toxin for many months and even years. Both types of algal bloom are enhanced by human industry such as mills and factories.

As much fun as it is to grab a snack right off the beach, a sobering reminder is that some people have died from eating just one clam. To date there is no reliable tests for detecting P.S.P's so eating shellfish is entirely at your own risk. I don't want to scare you away from the experience of eating shellfish you find along the paddling trail, just a few things to consider first.

I was kayaking in Barkley Sound on the west side of Vancouver Island not so long ago, and a short distance from our camp was an abundant bed of oysters. The bed was huge and I had sampled them before with no ill effects. A buddy of mine and I gathered about a dozen good size specimens and in camp, to the horrified faces of those who thought raw oyster sucking was disgusting, we sucked a few down. They were delicious! I was optimistically certain of their safety as I had eaten some from that spot a year earlier, but in hindsight, you never really know for sure. Anything in the environment of that area could have changed in the interim, and that happy oyster patch may have been contaminated by an aggressive bloom season. A year later in Desolation Sound I was witness to a member of another kayaking group sharing my island campsite who was recovering from a bad reaction to a clam. His throat began to close and for a time we were afraid things might become dire. His breathing was fine and after a few anxious hours, he returned to normal. It was close.

Odds are that you will be safe. Just consider the time of year. Take note of posted signage about prohibited harvesting areas, and remember that it is safer to harvest these filter fish during months that contain the letter R is not always reliable. The idea is that during these months the waters are cooler in temperature and less likely to give life to algal blooms of any kind. This is a false assumption. If you do decide to chance a fresh shellfish dinner try to harvest in areas well away from human industry. Logging zones, pulp mills, factories and fish farms all can contribute to the overall health of a bloom. I have included a nice recipe for oysters!

A Plan, a Floaty Plan!

Does anyone know where you are going this weekend? It is good practice to prepare a float plan even if you are just heading out for a quick weekend camping trip. Things happen out there, no matter how much planning we do. Giving someone back home a good idea of where you may be, and how you are getting there will help should something go terribly wrong and a search is initiated on your behalf. Pick a person you know. Preferably someone who is not currently the beneficiary to your life insurance policy. Preferably someone who also kayaks regularly and understands some of the challenges and changing conditions you will face on your trip. Carry a copy of your float plan with you in your kayak, which includes the following information.

>Your name.
>Date.
>Home Phone #.
>Make and colour of your car.
>Phone # of your emergency contact person.
>Your launch site.
>Destination and route (route if possible).
>Your return date.
>A time to call for a search (usually 24 hours beyond your estimated return time)
>Number of people in your group.
>Type and colour of your kayak (s).
>Your cell phone number (if applicable).

A few other things to remember about making a float plan. Factor in a bit of elbow room in your estimated times so that delays, minor ones, will not be cause to alarm the troops back home and be cause for an unnecessary search and rescue. If you are overdue for reasons out of your control then do your best to call your contact person or the authorities as soon as possible. Last minute changes to your float plan before or during your trip should be reported as well in a timely fashion. Make sure your contact has an answering machine, or voice mail and will check it regularly while you are away. Remember too that unnecessary searches cost us all in time and stress, not to mention monetary costs of launching a search and rescue operation. Good communications and contacts will lessen the likelihood of anyone jumping the gun to save you when you are just hanging out on a beach for an extra night.

The use of cell phones in the outdoors work well in most recreational areas on the west coast, as well as carrying a VHF marine transceiver will aid in checking in as needed. If your phone does not work, place a call to the local coast guard station with the radio. They will be happy to assist you in connecting with your contact person, and or, relay messages that you are fine. They will not assist you in getting a pizza delivered. They get right uppity when you try that. One last thing, don't be afraid of calling for help. I have heard tragic tales that all came down to ego. No one needs to go looking for epics. It has been my experience that they will find you. Once that happens better bet your buddy back home has a current location for you, and that is solely up to you!

> Tips:
> Peanuts are used in the manufacture of dynamite!

Keeping it clean!

Simple steps to proving you don't exist, or leaving little trace that you were ever there.

I remember being a child, growing up on an island. It seems long ago, or was it this morning. No, wait, that was not being a child, that was being childish and I don't want to delve too deeply into that episode. However, when I was younger I was an enlightened little guy. I suppose living so close to nature and living things of all sizes this affected me to being somewhat of an environmental Zen master by the age of six. I held tightly to a belief that nothing in nature should ever be moved, not one little inch. I would recoil at the thought of shifting even the smallest of pebbles. It was not right. It, the pebble belonged where it lay, and was there for a reason.

It was not as though the pebble in question had been there for an eternity. Change and slow motion movements are the basic ways of the earth, and its coating of nature in the ooze layer in which we all live. By the state of the world we live in, I would toss in the idea that change and slow motion also applies to human behaviour. At six I felt that a 'live and let live, leave and let be' approach was best. The one who does not bother a bee will not be stung; one should leave rocks alone to. Though, it seems in my forties I have relaxed the rules a bit and have retired to a less rigid way of coexisting with the natural world. This is real progress for the child-like environmental Zen master. The underlying methods of my youthful madness I still apply to camping in the delicate confines of the rainforest floor, and inter-tidal zones of the west coast. Plants, trees (standing and fallen) and yes, even those pesky pebbles are where they are for a reason. Nature works in wonderfully mysterious ways that we seem obsessed with conquering.

A rock landed where it is due to a glacier snipping off a chunk of coastal mountain twenty-million-years ago give or take five minutes, and depositing it on the beach as the glacier ceased to advance. It should not be disturbed. By now, you are wondering if I, your kayaking guide to a nice weekend of good food and camping under the stars is slightly disturbed. I do move rocks from time to time, but not without the knowledge for the tremendous damage done by doing so. That rock, long ago plopped down, or pushed up from below is now shelter to a minute eco-system. Plants for instance use the rock to grow behind, over and especially under. The rock gathers and provides tiny amounts of water, and rich nutrients to feed its garden. Moving this rock to pitch my tent is a disaster on the scale of a hurricane to those that live in and around a beach rock. I am not so fanatical that I would plant 'Do not Touch' signs on each stone I come across, though at the age of six I may well have.

Here are a few steps to consider when perfecting your invisible camping style. First, when you land on the beach stretch your legs by searching for the ideal camping spot. Make sure that it is the least intrusive and will end your stay with minimal impact to the wild plants that are there. Public marine parks, which will be your most likely destination by kayak, offer good places to pitch a tent and often provide raised beds and platforms for that purpose. If you are 'bushing it', do take care. You may not think that a day or two of tromping about will do much lasting damage, but it does. Most things revive after we camp, but some do not. You will notice for instance that a well-trafficked area has little or no growth around it. Concentrate your camping in established areas.

When choosing a camp make sure it is fairly level and large enough to accommodate you, your gear and your kayak(s). Choose a spot well above the high tide line and if possible inland from the shore for added shelter.

Avoid any potential problems handed out by Mother Nature. Pitch your camp away from steep slopes with loose material, dead trees, and areas with visible fresh evidence of animal tracks.

Keep it clean.

Picking up after yourself as you go along your daily routine, especially around dinnertime and cooking. This is a good routine to get into out there to avoid luring in critters into your kitchen area and into your camp in general. The animals are out there, even in public areas. The most destructive of all is not a bear, wolf, cougar or even mischievous raccoons, but the smallest of all, mice!

In one night, I lost the mesh pocket of my PFD due to a discarded granola bar wrapper I had left in it. A small dry bag had been carefully nibbled for no other reason than rodents are notorious vandals. Lastly, my water bag was nearly empty by morning because I had left it on the ground. A small hole chewed in it resulting in a fire hose flash flood that probably swept the surprise little mousey criminal away. Hanging food and water would have prevented this.

To rig up a food cache is relatively easy. Find a tree that has a solid healthy branch at least 15 feet off the ground. This is a good measurement especially in bear country. Use a 30 – 50 foot rope, or cord. At one end, attach something heavy, a carabineer will do. Throw that end up and over the branch and let if come close to the ground. Tie your bag to that end and pull your bag up, then tying off the other end of the line to the tree trunk.

Following my basic food packaging methods will reduce the amount of loose garbage that will gather in camp. Any pre-packaged food should be removed from its original packing at home, and put into Ziploc bags, remembering of course to label what they are. I always come home with a big Ziploc bag filled with others. Often they can be reused as well.

Packing out what you packed in is the mantra of no trace camping. Hang up your garbage bags as well. Alternatively, you can stow your food in the kayak's hatches at night. If doing this, remember where you are. If camping in bear areas, always hang up your food. The last thing you want to see in the morning is a mangled kayak ripped apart by a curious and hungry bear. In other cases, when it is just rodents and raccoons to worry about the hatches will do in a pinch. Making sure that the food is well sealed and in airtight dry bags. Leave nothing in your kayak's cockpit. Even with the cover on, they will find a way in. Once in the early hours I as broken from my slumber by rustling outside my tent. Most of the time sounds outside are exaggerated when laying in a tent, but this time it was something enough to get me up. I poked my head out the door to see three raccoons in the cockpit of my friend's kayak. The cover half removed and the little bandits were gobbling up his favorite snacks. Chasing the mob away proved silly, as they were now wise to the fact that we were a possible source of easy food. Never, I mean never bring food, even sealed food into your tent!

There is one item that cannot be neglected and has a very large impact on the environment, which is we all have to poop. Most established marine campgrounds provide outhouses. Occasionally, while camping in less established spots I have found the joke that someone considered to be a quality outhouse. Usually terrifying to enter! If there are no facilities available, the no-trace camper will have to decide how far to take things in this regard. Some forego toilet paper all together and rummage for some nice soft absorbent moss. Others need their two-ply. I lean towards the latter. Toilet paper is a big problem out there. Like walking the dog, you can bag it up and pack it out with you. Or, make sure it is burned completely. Digging a cat hole is a good idea if you are in a place that can accommodate this method. It should be away from trails, camp and fresh water supplies. Peeing is also something to think about. Wade into the ocean is best as human urine can attract some animals into camp while scaring others away.

Use existing fire pits or set up your own fire below the high tide line, and try to keep it small. (see camp fires).

One last item, before leaving your site make one last check after the boats are packed. I call this my, 'idiot check'. Scan your eyes over your campsite for anything you may have brought with you and any bits of garbage left behind. I also tend to repeat this idiot check on the beach as well prior to departing. Do your best to leave your camp spot the way it was when you found it. In a public park, we do this because the next paddler after us will appreciate it, and in the bush, all of nature will thank you.

Setting up your kitchen.

Pick a spot at least 20 feet from where you have pitched your tent. This way, if anything should wander in at night sniffing around where you have been cooking it will be far enough away from where you are sleeping. Remember, and I cannot stress this tidbit enough, do not for any reason bring food, snack, drinks etc. into your tent at night, or during the day. There is no seal tight enough to hold back food smell. This is what attracts animals into our camps in the first place. Cooking on the beach is perfect. The setting could not be more appealing, there are rocks and convenient logs everywhere to set up your kitchen. Take a look at your tide tables first. Check the wash marks on the beach that is the line of seaweed and debris washed up by the previous high tide. This is very important to know because should you turn in before the high tide reaches its peak and washed away your kitchen. Make sure it is all packed away securely well above that line. Your tide table will tell you whether it is an increasingly higher tide or if it is waning each day lower than that line.

Washing dishes may seem a benign thing to do. Again, you are playing in someone else's house while camping in the outdoors. The inter-tidal zone is a tough monkey. It takes a beating from stormy seas, and it is bashed by incoming debris. Pebbles from the beach tumble and roll over it day and night. We stomp about in our sandals and dump our dishwater onto these marine life habitats. Use of biodegradable soaps is a matter of pride and be careful about where you dump it. I don't bring a tub to wash dishes but do them individually at the shoreline using only small amounts of soap, and using crushed shell or sand to do most of the scrubbing. Avoid dumping your entire wash load over rocks or delicate areas on the beach. You are doing more harm than you know. It is better to disperse your soapy water on outgoing tides where it will be disperse widely and do far less harm than if deposited in a small area.

In performing a weekend of no-trace camping, a six-year-old's methods make for a good mindset. We can fool ourselves into thinking that by paddling a kayak and camping on the land, we do no harm. We enter this with the full intentions of being eco-minded but our very presence changes the places we visit. Before you begin rolling rocks to make room for your nylon abode, take a little walk. Stretch your legs after a long paddle and find a less intrusive place to camp out. By no means do I suggest we all tiptoe about out there, Mother Nature is not made of fine crystal, just remember who was there first.

Campfires!

Whether you are camping in a public park or in the wilderness, a fire can be a pleasant blessing, a comfort, and troublesome all at the same time. In my circle of kayakers, we have an unspoken campfire etiquette, keep it small. There are two camps when it comes to campfires. One side doesn't see the need to have one a campfire at all, especially in summer when the evenings are warm anyway. They are a hazard in summer months and the gathering of firewood can be a problem. The other camp sticks a tongue out at these fuddy-duddy party poopers and has a campfire any time. Those that do choose the fire route often do things that don't groove with good fire etiquette. There are a few simple, common sense rules to choosing a fire site, starting a fire, maintaining and caring for the fire, and what happens after you are gone.

Keeping it small is keeping it efficient. I spent a nice pair of nights at a place called, Garden Point. It is on Nootka Island at the intersection of Esperanza and Espinosa Inlets. A great spot to wait out a windstorm and it has an outhouse, well, sort of, and at the time, there were rumours of a troublesome bear that has learned some bad habits from us. All of that aside Garden Point also had a pre-existing fire pit. The thing was huge and filled to overflowing with ash and garbage and abused by others to the point that it was of no use to anyone else. This is at the root of common sense kayaking and camping. What you do today affects those that follow tomorrow. A fire pit that big under the low branches of the surrounding trees, mostly highly flammable entities, was a bad idea to start with. My paddling friend and I assessed the pit and decided on the following.

What we did next has shaped how we make our fires since. Mainly due to the disgust at the nasty bigger and unnecessary fire pits. We plucked stones from the wall around the existing pit, releasing small avalanches of ash as we did so. Then, placed the stones in a smaller semi-circle against the outside of the pit wall. When our newly constructed fire pit was complete, it looked from above like a turtle with our small cook fire being the head. We fed our infant fire with small sticks and twigs found on the ground. In fact, foraging for more wood was not an issue. We ran the little fire with what we gathered from the ground around camp for two days. No sawing, no eye-burning smoke from wet salty driftwood, just a small, incredibly hot fire. It served us well. From that day forth we vowed to make our fire pit so small that we could place our grill top on them. No more balancing acts with kabobs and the like, and it takes less energy to run a smaller campfire. They are just as aesthetic as any huge bon fire on the beach could be. In the morning, reigniting the fire took only a few handfuls of twigs and some lungpower as the ash and coals underneath were still quite hot.

Making a fire.

This is the age-old trick. The cave man that invented the stuff probably did it only the one time and by sheer accident. It was probably another fifty-million years before some other cave man accidentally started another fire. He did it by tossing out a cigarette while riding a woolie mammoth. It astonishes me how easily it is to start a forest fire by accident and so tremendously difficult to deliberately start a campfire.

The Boy Scouts teach this stuff where you do all manner of bizarre, sweaty techniques rubbing things on things. Bows, strings, flints sparking on bits of sphagnum and dried. moss. Then one young smart tike brought along some pitch. I have used pitch, the stuff is amazing. Though, there are many other ways to get those twigs alight. I bring my own firewood in the kayak. It is dry and what is to be found on the beach is not. A good supply of kindling wrapped in a garbage bag and tucked under the bungees is not much more to deal with on a short trip. I use this wood to start and maintain a fire while drying out 'found' wood. Fire starters are easy to make, and bought commercially. Most camping supply stores will sell some kind of paraffin-based fire starter. Bees wax is best. It burns longer and hotter. I use tea light candles, which I bring anyway for camp decorations and for my lanterns. They will sit nicely under your twigs and sticks and stay lit. They will also melt onto other things and keep the flames going. Cotton balls soaked in Vaseline works well too. And believe it or not, a tampon will make for a good fire starter. Simply unwrap it, pull it apart and put a match to it. Then, as with any other fire igniter add your kindling in three stages.

First you will need a supply of dry grass or very small twigs. Once you have a flame add more slowly being careful not to smother your infant fire. Then adding larger pieces until you have established a good fire. Another method is to build a twig structure around where the fire will start. A small tee-tee or my personal favorite, a box of interlocked sticks which will heat up and fall into the flames and creating a good bed of coals. When you have established a good coal bed then you are ready to cook. Just like at home with the BBQ once the coals are rippling with heat then you can start your steaks, kabobs ore whatever you want to grill. After your dinner is done, add medium sized pieces of wood and grow your campfire turning it into a pleasant entity to sit around until bedtime.

Having a fire near your camp can be pleasant just remember where you are. The tree liter on the ground is highly flammable as are branches above. Avoid gathering logs from the beach. Before about 125 years ago, driftwood as we see it now did not exist on the coastal beaches, other than some windfall and broken branches littering the shoreline. All the logs you find partly buried on the beaches are from logging activity on the coast. They are most likely runaways from log booms and could be permeated with creosote.

Cooking on your fire is grand. Campfire cooking is wise done away from your tent, at least 15 feet. It is best to set your fire down on the beach whenever possible. Below the high tide line so that the ocean takes care of any embers still clinging to life after you turn in for the night. They can be sneaky. I have seen a fire I had thought to be a completely dowsed reignite to full glory only five minutes after I had wrapped myself up in my sleeping bag. The ground and the fire pit's stone surround are very efficient at holding heat. Any partly burned wood may have a red ember core still going though the outside looks black and dead. Another reason to build your fire below the tide line is that the inter-tidal zone is hardier than the other bio-zones. When it comes time for bed, dowsing your fire as best as you can, then get up and check periodically just to make sure. It is the price you pay for that fun evening roasting marshmallows. Before I go on, a small tip about roasting marshmallows. First, when the mallow is melting on your stick try not to use that hand to gesture with while talking around the campfire. Your camp companions will not appreciate comets of molten sugar flying through the air. Second tip; dip your marshmallow in Baileys Irish Cream after roasting.

A good no-trace campfire can be made by lining the bottom of the pit with flat rocks and stones. The bigger, the flatter, the better. Raising them on logs or bits of driftwood will protect the ground underneath from the effects of heat and will leave the earth undisturbed. Line rocks around them and make your fire as usual. When dismantling it later, scatter the rocks back where you found them and toss the flat ones on the beach to cool, be careful as they will still be hot to the touch even the next day. Under your fire, you will find very little has changed. The last time I used this method all that remained was a small pile of spilled ash that filtered down between the stones. Not one blade of grass was singed. Remember before starting a campfire to choose your fire site well, making sure that it is level and flat, away from low branches and that you first remove any loose debris from the ground such as leaves and twigs.

Okay, so the weather has gone bad and a kayaking day has been turned into another day in camp. You are waiting for better weather to come with time on your hands. Here is what to do with that time. Build a sauna! I am sure that there are a myriad of ways to construct an outdoor camping sauna. A simple lean-too A-frame style using poles at the center to hold up the tarps. A Tee-Pee would work as well. That I will leave up to you and the ingenuity you will use in your own camp.

What you will need for the basic sauna is:

Rocks and stones. Making sure they are not from riverbeds or bedrock as those rocks may contain water. When heated the water turns to steam, steam wants to escape from within the rock and it will explode, which is hardly relaxing!

Tarps, bigger the better.

Firewood.

A nearby water supply.

Mark out the spot you want to build your sauna and build your frame making sure that the inside dimensions are large enough to accommodate you and anyone else and leaving room between you and the stone pile. Now bring in your stones and build a pile making sure to leave room under it for your fire. Build your fire and keep it burning for several hours or however long it will take to your stones thoroughly. It is important to get these stones hot as when the water is poured on them the outside of the rocks will cool, and the inner stones will continue to heat the pile. DO NOT start your fire in the covered sauna. Building the tarp covering for your sauna and then building a fire inside is both uncomfortable and possibly dangerous. Most beach wood is permeated with sea salt and will be very smoky when burning. This smoke would linger inside the enclosure.

After your rocks are heated, remove all the ash and coals from under the pile. Now you can cover your frame with the tarps. Climb in, splash some water on the hot stones, and enjoy. Keep a bucket of water in the sauna and try to pour the water on the same spot each time. Alternate chilling, I mean heating in the sauna with stepping out into the cold, or taking a dip in the ocean. This is an ultimately easy and luxurious way to spend an evening after paddling.

> Tips:
> Cover your cooking area with tarps strung on poles or between trees.

Some last words of advice for the weekend paddler

Share and Share Alike.
Coexisting with other paddlers, and the wildlife.

In recent years, the wilderness areas that until now had not seen a single Teva sandal footprint are being encroached upon. As kayaking has grown from a fringy sport to the throngs of paddlers there are now, these wilder places, some the last of their kind began to shrink. It is the same old story. The locals putting up with the tourists, in this case the locals are the local wildlife, as kayakers approached in their paddling pods spooking baby seals back into the ocean, eagles were scared away from meals, outraged sea lions flopped to the sea from rocky perches, at times abandoning or even trampling pups on the way. Sea birds few the coop leaving vulnerable nests and chicks to less intimidated predators. All these cases due to the false belief we kayakers have adopted that we are sustainable, we are quiet, we are not intrusive and low-impact visitors. Our paddles do nothing. They do not make a sound as they swish through the sea unlike motor boat propellers. We embrace no-trace camping etiquettes, but they should never be confused with no-impact camping, and for some time we paddlers were not doing our part. Toilet paper and pop top cans, wrappers and scraps all left behind. Slowly however the ethic of wilderness camping has changed. The tone is now more in the favour of the wilderness, not our selfish need for wilderness experiences. What we do out there affect both those living in the natural world, and those campers and wilderness seekers that come after us.

Clean the beaches, clean the water

Everytime I come home from a paddle day or trip I seem to have a big bag of garbage. This bag was not filled with wrappers and debris created from my own cooking and camping, but garbage I have found while on my paddling travels. Mostly bottles, bags and wrappers. Take on a routine of doing this. If you see something that does not belong on the beach, or in the water, or in the woods pick it up, bag it and bring it home. Some of my most wonderful finds still adorn my bookshelf. A large red port light bulb I found bobbing in the water near Clayoquot Sound I scooped up thinking it a Japanese glass fishnet float. Alas, it was not that, but as garbage goes, it is unique. Being a no-trace kayaker goes beyond just tidying up after yourself.

Them and Us

No matter how silent, the kayaker is intrusive, perhaps to a lesser extent than other means of traveling but we do step onto beaches, trample over inter tidal zones and pitch out campsites in the untouched and delicate regions of the forests. To reconnect with nature is why we paddle to these places but it is on all our shoulders, a shared responsibility to preserve and protect. To do this, start by adopting a no-trace camping etiquette that I have presented in this book. Leave nothing out to attract wildlife in. We are on their turf and have been responsible for teaching some of them some very bad habits. Don't go out there asking them to adapt to our needs and behavior. That is simply a wrong and arrogant approach. We must adapt to where we are and where they exist.

Distance is crucial in co-existing with wildlife. It is always our deepest wish while paddling to have encounters with seals, whales and all the rest of them. They don't feel the same way. Legally, we must stay at least 100 yards from marine life, and even further away from approaching whale pods. Should an orca pod come towards you, get out of the way, and if they are moving too fast, stay put. Coming close to a colony of seals or seal lions will end in panic for them and perhaps some unwanted encounters for you as well. Seals are especially skittish and though I have been a long way away from a mother and pup, it seems inevitable that they will scatter and dive into the water. I feel for them. Seals are not the best parents either. I have witnessed an adult seal leap back into the water, leaving the pup alone on the rocks. When we paddle, we are seen as predators, or bigger competition to the food. Don't be fooled, we are not welcome. Just because we come in low-impact vehicles does not mean we are seen as a natural part of things. Be wary and be patient. Bring a pair of binoculars in your cockpit bag and a camera with a good zoom lens. Remembering that some of the most memorable experiences on the water are those you hold in your mind's eye.

Getting along with your fellow campers can be as arduous as dealing with the local wildlife. However, one simple rule of thumb still applies, distance from wildlife is one thing, distancing yourself from other people may be harder to accomplish. One gets more with honey than with vinegar and a congenial approach to those who have arrived before you will make the invasion of you and your group easier to for them to bear. We all go out looking for that solitude and wilderness experience like no other. The fact is no one should paddle into a public marine park setting expecting it to be wild, untamed and devoid of people. My experiences even out in the wilds of the coast have had me inviting the neighbours over for some campfire chat after dark. We are never alone, whether surrounded by campers, tents and chatter or by creatures in the woods sneaking about in the darkness. Co-existing with the local wildlife is the easy part. Don't bother them and most likely they will leave you well enough alone as well. People on the other hand are a bit dodgy.

I have examples both good and fulfilling to terribly awkward encounters with my fellow paddling travelers. These occurred in settings of tight camping locations leaving little room in between. In one instance, I came in from a lovely evening paddle at sunset to find someone had pitched their tent so close to mine that our tent pegs were sharing the same holes. The person in question, an older woman paddling solo appeared from her tent like a spooked bear and before I could say one disgruntled word, she apologized for having to be so close and offered me lukewarm beer. I had to laugh and in the end, that became one of the most pleasant and memorable evenings as others bumped elbows along the small beachfront, she and I tapped beer cans and admired the view.

A second example is one that deteriorated and in the end was never resolved fully. On landing on one of the most coveted locations in a west coast marine park my group was met with someone camping on the beach. He was someone we knew from home and assumed that out arrival would be welcomed. It was not. A discussion at the campfire resulted in his insistence that we were deliberately intruding upon his privacy by camping so close. In his mind, we should have seen him there and gone elsewhere. Perhaps he had a point it was a small area. We made offers to move by morning if the other group further up the campsite left as planned, but that was not good enough. The discussion was not pleasant, and long-winded. We did move by morning but not before a second angry volley from our neighbour over breakfast. It was getting out of hand and no matter what concessions were made in his direction, he wanted us gone.

In our defense, he did not make things easy on himself. First, he had taken three tent-spots for and refused to consolidate his gear to make room. He had also been there much longer than the permitted days per campsite. It had become Fortress Island to him. Keep out was his message to anyone coming ashore. An unrealistic viewpoint to hold in a public setting, and when we returned from our paddling day he was gone, and a nasty note pinned to our tent, a tent we had moved at breakfast under his watchful eye. We had poured honey all over this fellow, but it turned rapidly to vinegar.

I will always welcome you in, I have warm beer and usually some tasty left-overs, good stories to share and a smile. Paddle in, try to shelve your disappointment at seeing someone already there and take on the same attitude. As for the wildlife, if you take a common-sense approach to camping in their living room and give them some peace of mind by keeping some distance between you and them, the honey should flow!

> Tips:
> Ziploc bags filled with water and frozen flat make excellent ice packs to help keep your fresh ingredients cool.

the kayak, and the kitchen

Stuffing the Hatches!

It never ceases to amaze me that whether it is a ten-day outing I am planning, or an overnight quickie, the basics are the same and I once again attempt to fit the same enormous pile of gear into my kayak's hatches. The only difference for a shorter journey to the outdoors is that the food bag is slightly smaller, but only just slightly.

Listed below are the basics that I might bring on a solo day, or overnight trip. This list is widely variable depending on the meals I plan to cook, the number of people that may be accompanying me and so on. When I started paddling, it was with a smaller kayak. I was forced by necessity to pare down what I brought, however; with the bigger touring kayak, that list grew with a few more toys added here and there. Bring only what you think you will need, as space is always an issue and sometimes, packing stuff in nooks and crannies is the only way to get it all to fit. Smaller dry bags are useful for this. Practice the packing of your kayak before the trip to streamline the task when the day comes.

A kayak-guiding friend referred to the hatch-filling task as the 'daily miracle', and with good reason. Believe it or not with some practice and routine it will all fit. I colour code my dry bags as well to make things easier still. The red 10L bag is for my camp clothing, the black 10L bag has the breakfast ingredients in it, etc. I use the same bags each trip for the same things and build my packing routine around them.

- A seaworthy kayak.
- PFD (personal floatation device).
- Paddling jacket.
- Sandals or booties.
- Spray skirt.
- Cockpit cover.
- Paddle.
- Spare paddle.

Paddle float.
Sponge.
Buoyant heaving line.
Bailing pump.
Deck light.

Cockpit Bag:

Money and car keys. (I hide a spare set somewhere on the vehicle just in case)
Sunglasses.
Sunscreen.
SPF rated lip balm.
Headlamp.
Toilet paper.
Camera.
First aid kit.
Flares and gun.
Binoculars.
Pocket knife.
Snacks.
Duct tape.
Guide book.
Charts and chart bag.

Travel Bag:

Spare clothing.
T-shirts.
Shorts.
Fleece jacket and pants.
Long sleeve shirt.
Rain gear (ya just never know!)
Toque.
Dry socks.
Book.
Spare batteries.
Candle lantern.

Food Bag:

Meals for duration of trip.
Snacks.
Toiletries, i.e. toothpaste, toothbrush, deodorants.

Spices.
Coffee and teas.
Dry ingredients.

Cooler Bag:

Meats.
Milk.
Veggies.
Sauces.

Kitchen Bag:

Stove.
Fuel.
Funnel.
Pot set.
Pot lid grabber.
Wok.
Utensils (can be carried in small kit box)
Dish towel.
Pot scrubber.
Bowls, plates, cups.
Garbage bags.
One cup coffee press.
(Espresso maker, optional).

Kit Box:

Utensils.
Funnel.
Duct tape.
Skewers.
Lighters.
Matches.
Tea light candles.
Spare batteries.

Water = at least ten litres. (Assuming a 2 night stay)

Camping Gear:

Tent.

Sleeping bag.
Inflatable sleeping pad (Therma-rest).
Candle lantern.
Headlamp.
Dry bags.
50 ft cord.

Kayak Kitchen Checklist.

Assuming you have such items in your cupboard as basil, oregano and thyme, chili powder and cayenne powder here are a few other things to bring along for flavourful outdoors cooking.

Fresh herbs – these are basil, oregano, dill weed, thyme, rosemary and mint leaves. All add something to your dishes. Fresh is best but dried will do. The ratio of fresh to dried is roughly 3 – 1. I.E. 3 tablespoons fresh = 1 tablespoon dried.

Bay leaves – add to soups and other dishes while simmering, but remember to remove them before serving.

Coriander – ground or whole, dried or fresh, but dried is never a substitute for fresh leaves.

Curry powder – is a blend of spices in Indian dishes.

Cumin – works well with chili powder in Mexican and middle-eastern dishes.

Garlic – used minced, crushed, or whole...fresh is best but you can get away with using powdered. I won't tell.

Red pepper flakes – adds heat to any dish, remember, less is more!

Turmeric – is an inexpensive alternative to saffron. It gives a pungent taste and a yellowish colour to dishes.

Stock – (veggie, chicken, or beef) usually there is no time to fuss about with making your own stock from scratch, but the powdered forms work well for me.

Olive oil – Go for the best extra virgin olive oils. It is expensive but you will taste the benefits.

Vegetable oil – Safflower, sunflower, and canola oils.

Jalapeno peppers – get them fresh for all your cooking needs, but be careful, they are hot and avoid rubbing your face!

Hot pepper sauces – Tabasco sauce is the most common brand but there are many others to experiment with just how hot is hot.

Ginger – Fresh or dried. Again fresh is best. Adding some ginger to your dishes, especially bean dishes and you will not toot again.

Wooden or Metal skewers – To be used with grilling over the campfire, or for use with dipping into fondue pots. I prefer the wooden skewers to the metal because they can be tossed in the fire and leave no trace. One less thing to clean and not to mention the pointy fact they are hard to pack.

Utensils.

Camp stove, single or double burner.

Pot set.

Water bag.

Plates, bowls and cups for mixing.

A few other optional items that make for a luxury evening in camp:

The GSI camp wok: This little piece of cookery has removed the use of one cook pot and fry pan from my kit bag. I have done numerous stir-fries in it as well as wok-pancakes in the morning. Available at most outdoors stores.

The GSI double shot espresso maker: Available in single and double sizes the coffee maker is very simple to use and takes minimal clean-up. It sits on a camp stove well and there is nothing finer than an espresso in camp.

At Home and in Camp...

Before we get all excited about preparing the yummy recipes, there are a few last little words of camp cooking advice I would like to pass on. I do this now, before the recipe pages as in many cases I would simply be repeating myself if I made these suggestions at the beginning of each recipe. Most of the ideas in the pages to follow are prepared partly at home and stuffed into Ziploc bags of varying sizes, while some can be prepared wholly in camp. It is up to you the humble kayaker and cook as to how much messing about you are prepared to deal with. Cooking from scratch is an art form and when adding the outdoors it goes a little further into the oddball side of things. You will not find flat kitchen counters out there, perhaps a picnic table if you wander into a marine park setting. Mostly, you will be faced with setting up your stove and pots on some wet log, or a rock with a slope. Be prepared for wind whipping your ingredients bags down the sand. Mother Nature loves messing with the camping chef and creating as much chaos as possible. Keeping a pebble supply on hand to hold down loose Ziplocs is a good idea.

It came to mind the other morning that preparing certain items well ahead of an outing made sense. I usually spend a few minutes in camp mixing veggie, or chicken stock powder, but why not blend a small container of it at home and stick it in the fridge for later. A small half-litre water bottle filled with ready to go vegetable stock is something I do now. On a weekender, doing this will speed things up in camp. Most of the veggies can be chopped, diced, julienned and so on at home. It is always nice to cut these up fresh in camp, however as a chopped bell pepper does get a little sad and withered after a few days out. Chop what you need for your first meal and then leave the rest for something to do on that lazy second afternoon. I don't mind spending that time before making dinner to slice things up. That said, a chopped up, sliced up, julienned up veggie will pack easier in your ingredients bag.

Many of my recipes call for chicken. This is something I was shy about doing in the beginnings of my kayak camping. Fear of a night of upset stomachs, vomiting or dying from chicken gone bad put me off. Nevertheless, for a weekend trip chicken is something that can come along and tastes great. Again, I leave it up to the cook, but if the weather looks to be on the hot side, or even if it is not, I like to pre-cook the chicken at home. Lightly sauté, or boiled at home, and then let it cool before packing it. Remember to adjust the cooking time in camp to compensate for this pre-cooking. Add the chicken later on in the camp cooking process.

So as the sun sinks down behind the trees get the water boiling and remember this one last fact...Don't panic, don't rush your cooking no matter how wobbly the wet log...camping is supposed to be a fun relaxing pastime, so enjoy

> Tips:
> To clean your grill rub it with a ball of aluminum foil.

Cooking Measurement Equivalents:

To date, I have not found the ability to measure the perfect 1/8 of a teaspoon and I seem to measure ingredients in clumps and pinches rather than with cups and spoons. For those of you who play by the rules I have come up with some general, rule of thumb equivalents...but to me, a pinch still hurts, and a dash is a short fast run.

16 tablespoons = 1 cup

12 tablespoons = 3/4 cup

10 tablespoons + 2 teaspoons = 2/3 cup

8 tablespoons = 1/2 cup

6 tablespoons = 3/8 cup

5 tablespoons + 1 teaspoon = 1/3 cup

4 tablespoons = 1/4 cup

2 tablespoons = 1/8 cup

2 tablespoons + 2 teaspoons = 1/6 cup

1 tablespoon = 1/16 cup

2 cups = 1 pint

2 pints = 1 quart

3 teaspoons = 1 tablespoon

48 teaspoons = 1 cup

breakies:

Here's the thing, I don't do breakfast. All I need for breakfast is black, piping hot liquid. I know, I know, it is the most important meal of the day and as an author of a cookbook, I should be promoting good nutrition and sensible eating habits, especially when physical excursion may be part of the day's agenda. The fact is, I opt out of breakfast and the only thing I want and can stomach seeing in the morning is my one-cup French press steeping some Salt Spring Coffee Co. Sumatran roast. Or even better the espresso maker on my camp stove squirting out something rich and dark. I will force down a pot of hot porridge on those paddling days that look long and gloomy. Double portions if the rain is sideways.

So, for you breakfast eating people I have added some favorites passed onto me by other breakfast eating people I know. That said, I would never turn down a banana pancake.

Asparagus Omelet

Eggs on camping trips are not easy, but can be done. Most outdoor stores supply egg carriers. The crucial thing with an egg in the outdoors is not to break it! Moreover, keeping it refrigerated. For an overnighter, this is a nice first morning treat. Another good way to bring eggs along is to hard-boil them before you go. A hard-boiled egg has perfect packaging. Not so good for omelet making, but nonetheless, a nice snack.

Makes 4 servings

Ingredients:

1 lb fresh asparagus spears, trimmed
5 eggs
2 tablespoons olive oil
2 tablespoons Parmesan cheese, shredded

Directions:

In camp:
Cook asparagus in salted boiling water for 5-10 minutes. Drain, and then cut into ½-inch lengths. In a bowl, beat eggs with a whisk and stir in asparagus. In a large non-stick, fry pan heat oil and pour in egg mixture, allowing settling and cook until almost set. Sprinkle with Parmesan and carefully fold in half with spatula, then cook for 2 minutes until browned on each side.

Buckwheat Pancakes

Makes 2 – 4 servings

Ingredients:
1 cup buckwheat flour
½ cup whole wheat flour
½ cup cornmeal
½ cup skim milk (added in camp)
2 teaspoons baking powder
1 teaspoon salt
2 tablespoons oil

Directions:

At home:
Place all ingredients in a Ziploc bag.

In camp:
Empty contents into a medium size pot or bowl, stir in 2 – 3 cups of water and add milk. Spoon into a hot oiled pan and cook until bubbles appear then flip and cook the other side until golden brown. Serve with a little of your favorite syrup, and try a little bit of sliced banana on top!

Corn Pancakes

Makes 2 servings

Ingredients:
¾ cup cornmeal
¾ cup whole wheat flour
½ cup raw wheat germ
½ cup skim milk (added in camp)
2 teaspoons baking powder
½ teaspoon salt
2 tablespoons oil
1 tablespoon honey

Directions:

At home:
Put contents in a Ziploc bag.

In camp:
Empty contents into a medium size pot. Stir in 1 ½ cups of water. Mix well and spoon into a hot oiled fry pan. Cook until bubbles appear in batter and then flip. Cooking both sides until golden brown. Serve with your favorite syrup.

French Toast

Makes 2 servings

Ingredients:
4 tablespoons dried egg powder, or 2 eggs
3 tablespoons milk
Pinch of salt
2/3 cup water
6 slices French bread

Directions:

In camp:
In a bowl, combine eggs or egg powder, milk and salt. Add water gradually and beat to prevent lumping. Dip bread into mixture and set aside. Allow liquid to soak in.
In a lightly greased hot frying pan, grill the bread until golden brown on both sides. Serve with syrup.

Camp Garbage

Ingredients:
1 can sweetened condensed milk
2 cups (or use your can) of rolled oats
2 diced apples
1 sliced banana
15 - 20 green grapes

Directions:
In camp:
Mix all the ingredients together, and eat! It sounds very sweet, but it is a quick sugar pick up, includes some nutritious aspects, and you can clean up very quickly from this morning side dish.

Go Banana Pancakes

Makes 4 – 6 servings

Ingredients:
1 cup flour
1 teaspoon sugar, white
2 teaspoons baking powder
¼ teaspoon salt
1 egg, beaten
1 cup milk
2 tablespoons vegetable oil
2 ripe bananas, mashed

Directions:

At home:
Mix together all dry ingredients in a Ziploc bag.

In camp:
In a bowl, combine flour, sugar, baking powder, and salt. In a separate bowl beat egg and mix in milk, veggie oil and mashed bananas. Stir flour mixture in with banana mixture; the batter will end up slightly lumpy. Heat non-stick pan and pour batter in using about ¼ cup per pancake. Cook until golden brown on each side and serve hot with syrup, and cream.

snacks:

Who can live without snacks? Here are some of the other foodstuffs I bring along other than pepperoni sticks, which are a tasty boost while paddling and so well preserved that they can last under the deck bungees all afternoon, covered in salt water and spray and still taste good. Bulk nuts, sesame crackers and chocolate bars come with me too, but it is fun to take one or two snack items that I have made myself beforehand.

In the following pages are some that can be made at home beforehand for convenience sake, and one or two that can be made along the watery way. Traditional Bannock being one that fills the empty corners and gives a reason to hang around the campfire telling tales like old voyageurs.

Anzac Cookies

Sit on a beach nibbling these and image you are in Gallipoli. I hope that it is less noisy and horrific! This is the Aussie recipe for the cookies sent to the men during World War I. They were still fresh after a two-month boat trip so they should last for a weekender in your kayaks.

Ingredients:
1 cup whole wheat flour
1 cup unsweetened coconut
1 cup brown sugar
1 cup rolled oats
½ cup butter
2 tablespoons water
½ teaspoon baking soda
1 tablespoon honey

Directions:

At home:
Combine flour, coconut, sugar, and oats in a large bowl. Mix well.
In a saucepan, melt butter with the water, soda and honey. Add this to dry ingredients and mix well with your hands. (yes this will be sticky work).
Shape into cookies and bake on an oiled cookie sheet at 350 degrees for 20 minutes or until brown. Cool on rack.

Bannock...oh Canada!

The History:
Bannock is a truly Canadian food, well not totally Canadian, but all Canadians should have the experience of making it. It is a common misconception that Europeans adapted this dish from a native recipe. In fact, it was the other way around as most native peoples did not have access to flour until contact with settlers. Bannock has origins in Scotland. Our country was settled by many different ethnic groups, therefore there more than one traditional recipe. Flour was a luxury item in the early days of the fur trade. It was used to thicken pemmican style soup, rubbaboo, or occasionally to make galettes. Galette is the name used by voyageurs of the North West Company for an unleavened flour-water biscuit made by baking in a frying pan, or in the ashes of the campfire. The Selkirk Settlers referred to their flour water biscuit as bannock. Eventually bannock became the name accepted and recorded in journals and diaries throughout the western interior of Canada. By the mid 1800's the original flour-water mixture became more elaborate with the addition of salt, suet, lard, butter, buttermilk, baking soda, or baking powder. Bannock acquired other names, too: bush bread, trail bread, or grease bread. The traditional way to prepare bannock was to mix the ingredients into a large round biscuit and bake in a frying pan or propped up against sticks by the campfire. Give it a go, eh!

Ingredients:
1 cup white flour
1/4 tsp. salt
1 tsp baking powder
1 tablespoon butter or margarine
1/3 cup or more cold water

Directions:

In camp:
Mix dry ingredients thoroughly then rub in butter until well blended. Add enough water to make thick dough. Form into 1-inch thick cakes and place in the bottom of a greased cast iron frying pan. Cook on low heat until done on both sides, or prop the pan in the coals of the campfire. For a variety, add dry fruits, raisins, blueberries, etc. For pancakes, simply add a couple of eggs, omit the butter and substitute water for milk. For native style use half white flour, and half corn flour. To avoid the mess when clean up is a problem, measure out individual portions into a Ziploc and knead the dough in the bag until done.

> Tips:
> The average person consumes about 1500 pounds of food per year.

Beer Fondue

Makes 3 – 4 servings

Ingredients:
2 cups cheddar cheese, grated
1 cup beer, preferably a pale ale (I will sacrifice one for the fondue cause)
1 clove garlic, crushed
2 tablespoons cornstarch
½ teaspoon dry mustard
French bread

Directions:

At home:
Shred the cheese and package it in a small Ziploc bag. Combine the mustard and cornstarch in a Ziploc bag. Save one can of beer (yes you have too!) and carry the garlic separately.

In camp:
In a cook pot, place the beer, cheese and garlic. If you have a heat diffuser this is a good time to use it. Another method to keep your fondue warm but not over-cooked is to fill a pot with some water, add a couple small stones, and place the fondue pot inside it. The stones will keep the pot lifted over the hot water and stop from scorching the cheese. Warm pot over low flame until cheese has melted. In a cup, blend in the cornstarch with some extra beer or a small amount of water. Add to fondue and stir until thickened.
Serve with chunks of French bread.

Black Beanie Brownies

Makes about 2 dozen one inch squares

Ingredients:
1 can black beans, rinsed and drained
3 eggs
3 tablespoons vegetable oil
¼ cup cocoa powder
1 pinch salt
1 teaspoon vanilla extract
¾ cup white sugar
½ cup chocolate chips (optional...but yummy)
Directions:

At home:
Preheat oven to 350 degrees. Lightly grease an 8 x 8 baking dish.
  Combine the black beans, eggs, oil, cocoa powder, salt, vanilla, and sugar in a food processor and blend until smooth. Pour mixture into baking dish. Sprinkle chocolate chips over the top of the mixture.
  Bake in preheated oven until top is dry and the edges start to pull from the sides of pan, about 30 minutes.

Chocolate Fondue

Ingredients:
12 oz dark chocolate
8 oz heavy cream
Treats to dip such as apple chunks (granny smiths are my favorite), grapes (they seem to hold the chocolate very well), berries, or banana chunks.
1 tablespoon Baileys Irish Cream, Amaretto, or Kirsch

Directions:

At home:
Grate, or shave chocolate into Ziploc bag.

In camp:
Here we get to use the double boiler method again. Hopefully, you have cook pots that nestle well one in the other. Fill the bottom pot with some water and set the second pot inside it over medium heat. If the pots don't sit well together add some beach stones of equal size into the water pot. I have left behind this method and bought a small tea-light candle powered fondue warmer with ceramic dish.

Warm the cream until little bubbles form. Add the chocolate and blend. Transfer chocolate pot away from flame. The chocolate can be re-heated if it starts to cool.

Arrange your dip-ables on a plate and using a wooden skewer dip each piece into the warm chocolate.

Energy Balls!

Ingredients:
1 cup chocolate chips
½ cup oatmeal
½ cup crunchy peanut butter
½ cup nuts, or sunflower seeds
1 tablespoon honey
Wheat germ

Directions:

At home:
Mix all ingredients into a bowl and make into small round balls about 1 inch in diameter. Roll lightly in wheat germ. Move to plate or cookie sheet and allow to set in refrigerator for 30 minutes.

Gorp

Ever wonder what gorp stood for? "Gorp" stands for "Good Old Raisins and Peanuts". It is a traditional mix taken on hikes and outings, and provides a great energy burst in the middle of physical activity. Everyone I've talked to has a different combination of ingredients which they like to include in their gorp. Here is mine:

Ingredients:
A selection of cashews, salted peanuts, and almonds
Raisins and currants
Sunflower seeds
Nuts and Bolts mix
Smarties
Dried apricots and banana chips

Directions:

At home:
Combine all ingredients in a Ziploc bag, and shake to mix everything up. Take gorp paddling in your cockpit bag and nibble whenever you need an energy burst!

Granola Bars

Combine:
3 cups rolled oats
1/2 cup flour
1 cup brown sugar
1 tsp. melted butter
1 tsp. vanilla

Directions:

At home:
Mix well. Press into a cookie sheet and bake at 350 F for 10 minutes or until golden. Cool and cut into bars.
Optional: you can also add 1/2 to 1 cup of whatever else you would like chopped nuts, chocolate chips, raisins, coconut, honey, etc.

Hummus, Alfalfa Sprouts and Cheese in a Pita

Ingredients:
Hummus - can be bought already made in the deli department
Alfalfa sprouts, sharp cheese, and pita breads.

Directions:

In camp:
Simply spread an even layer of hummus on a pita and combine all ingredients into a sandwich, and enjoy!

Rolling Waves Choco-oat Bars

Makes approx. 24 bars

Ingredients:

¾ cup butter
½ cup brown sugar
½ cup honey
1 teaspoon vanilla
1 cup dried apricots, chopped
1 cup currants or raisins
1 cup unsweetened coconut, shredded
½ cup walnuts, chopped
1 cup almonds, slivered
½ cup rolled oats
1 cup wheat germ
2 cups chocolate chips
1 egg

Directions:

At home:
In a small saucepan, melt butter. Add brown sugar, honey and vanilla, stirring well to mix. Set aside to cool. In a large bowl, combine all fruits, nuts, and grain and chocolate chips. In a small bowl, beat egg. Stir it into butter mixture and drizzle over dry ingredients. Mix thoroughly. Press into a greased 9 x 13 inch cake pan. Bake at 325 degrees for 45 minutes. Let cool. Cut into 24 bars about ½ inch by 3 inches. Wrap each one in wax paper and pack in large Ziploc bag.

Sesame Seed Cookies

Ingredients:
1 cup sesame seeds
½ cup unsweetened coconut, grated
2 eggs
½ cup oil
½ cup honey
1 teaspoon vanilla
2 ¼ cups whole-wheat flour
½ teaspoon salt

Directions:

At home:
In a pan over medium/high heat, toast sesame seeds and coconut until lightly browned; stir often!

Combine eggs, oil, honey, and vanilla, and then stir in seeds and coconut.

Blend in the flour and salt, and stir well. Form dough into balls about an inch in diameter and place on a cookie sheet, press down on each with fork. Bake at 325 degrees for 15 minutes.

wraps:

Wrap it Up!

Wraps are a good way to make a lunch from leftovers. Often a batch of rice will get too big and I will use it to make wraps for the next day. Here are a few ideas for wraps on the go, and the ingredients can be organized ahead of time.

Chicken, avocado and Bacon

Makes 4 wraps.

Ingredients:
1 ripe avocado, halved, pitted and peeled
4 tortilla wraps
½ lb cold cooked chicken breast, thinly sliced
4 thin slices bacon, cooked and crumbled. (pre-packaged bacon bits will do)

Directions:

At home:
Slice chicken thinly and in batches cook over medium heat in an oiled pan until lightly browned on all sides and cooked through. Allow to cool and put in a Ziploc bag.

In camp:
Mash avocado with a fork, or slice thinly. Spread over tortillas. Top with chicken and bacon. Season to taste. Roll them up crosswise and cut in half.

Flood Tide Fajitas!

Makes 2 servings

Ingredients:
2 boneless, skinless chicken breasts, or 1 medium size steak
2 bell peppers, cut into thin strips
2 onions, cut into thin rings, then halved
1 zucchini, cut into thin strips
1 can chipotle pepper salsa
1 package soft tortilla wraps
Chili powder
Salt and black pepper to taste

Directions:

At home:
Cut chicken, or steak into thin strips. You can pre-cook the meat at this point if you wish. Place strips in a large Ziploc bag with a dollop of the salsa. Seal once all air is removed and refrigerate.

In camp:
Prepare the veggies and in a dry pan-fry the onions over high heat for 5 minutes. They will burn a bit, don't worry that adds flavour. Season with chili powder, salt and pepper to taste while frying. Add meat, peppers and zucchini and continue to sauté on high heat for 5 more minutes. The veggies should appear crisp.

To serve, add a row of chicken pieces, or beef to the center of each tortilla and pile on the veggies. Add some sour cream and the salsa. Enjoy.

Peanut Butter and Banana Wrap

If you have made the banana pancakes found in the 'breakies' section for breakfast, you may have a banana or two laying about taking up space in your hatch. I know, bananas are cumbersome and heavy. They don't pack well in limited space and that is why I rarely consider them to be good kayaker food items. But, I love my bananas. For a short weekend outing, I have room for them. In addition, there is nothing better than a filling peanut butter and banana wrap in the middle of a paddling day. Good energy source as well.

Makes 4 wraps

Ingredients:
4 tortilla wraps
4 tablespoons chunky peanut butter
3 - 4 ripe bananas, mashed
2 tablespoons honey

Directions:

In camp:
Spread tortillas with peanut butter. Top with mashed bananas and drizzle honey over it all. Roll up and slice in half.

Tuna Wrap

Makes 4 wraps

Ingredients:
6 cans tuna in mayo with corn
2 teaspoons horseradish
4 tortilla wraps
1 red bell pepper, seeded and cut into thins strips
1 green bell pepper, seeded and cut into thin strips

Directions:

At home:
Combine tuna with ¼ cup mayonnaise and ¼ cup corn. Keep cool.

In camp:
Combine tuna with horseradish. Spread mixture on tortillas. Top with bell pepper strips. Roll up and cut in half.

soups:

I love making soups and use them on my trips all the time. This section of the Hungry Kayaker one of the larger and deciding which of my favorites to leave out was a daunting task...perhaps there will be a Hungry Kayaker II, Revenge of the Soups!

There is nothing more refreshing than a steaming bowl of soup after a typical day of kayaking. Whether it is an afternoon outing or a longer multi-day event on the water a bowl of soup hits the spot. It is not much bother to plan a soupy lunchtime treat, and all it requires is the forethought of bringing a single burner stove and something to light it with, a pot, a bowl and a spoon. I have included a few of my favorites in this section along with a few that require a crock pot. If you do not have one, go out right now and buy one, they are wonderful inventions for soup and stew making at home.

Some of the recipes state the use of dried ingredients, but those can be exchanged for fresh if you are making it from scratch at home, and not in camp. Most often, soups are something I will make at home rather than wasting time and camp fuel in camp. Soups are good for ease of use on kayaking trips and making a selection of soups at home prior to a trip is a good plan. When the soup is cooled, I pour it into Ziploc freezer bags and lay them flat in the freezer. A good tip is to use a cookie sheet for this. A flat soup is easier to pack than a blob of frozen soup. As a bonus, this frozen soup helps keep any of your fresh fruits and veggies cool in the food bags as well.

Basic Backpacker Chili...also good for kayaking

Makes 4 servings
Cooking time in crock pot 2 - 3 hours

Ingredients:
½ lb. ground beef
½ lb. sausage cut into thin slices
½ cup onion, chopped
½ lb. mushrooms, sliced
¼ cup celery, chopped
¼ cup green bell pepper, chopped
1 cup salsa
1 16oz. can tomato juice
1 6 oz. can tomato paste
½ teaspoon sugar
½ teaspoon salt
½ teaspoon dried oregano
½ teaspoon Worcestershire sauce
¼ teaspoon dried basil
¼ teaspoon pepper

Directions:

At home:
In a fry pan brown sausage, ground beef and onion, then as the meat becomes brown add mushrooms, celery, and green pepper. Continue cooking and add remaining ingredients. Pour contents of pan into slow cooker, cover and cook on high for 2 to 3 hours.

Blue Jellyfish and Celery Soup

Makes 4 servings

Ingredients:
4 celery stalks, chopped.
3 ½ cups chicken broth.
1 cup crumbled blue cheese (if blue jellyfish are not in season).
2 – 3 tablespoons light cream.
Ground black pepper to taste.

Directions:

At home:
In a large saucepan, cook celery in simmering broth for 20 minutes. Transfer to blender or food processor and puree until smooth. Return to pan and add cheese. Heating gradually, stirring until cheese melts.

Allow to cool and pour into Ziploc bags. In camp, reheat and divide into 4 serving bowls.

Just Plain Chicken Stew

Makes 4 servings
Cooking time in crock pot 8 – 10 hours

Ingredients:
1lb. boneless, skinless chicken breast, cubed
1 14oz. can diced tomatoes
2 potatoes, peeled and cubed
5 carrots, chopped
2 celery sticks, chopped
1 onion, chopped
2 small cans mushroom stems and pieces, drained
2 teaspoons chicken stock
2 teaspoons sugar
½ teaspoon dried basil
1 teaspoon chili powder
¼ teaspoon pepper
1 tablespoon cornstarch
1 cup water

Directions:

At home:
Combine all ingredients except cornstarch and water into slow cooker. Mix water and cornstarch, stir into slow cooker. Cover and cook on low for 8 to 10 hours until vegetables are tender.

Chunky Pizza Soup

Makes 2 servings

Ingredients:
1 tbsp vegetable oil
small onion, chopped
1/2 cup sliced mushrooms
1/4 cup sweet green pepper, chopped
1 28 oz can plum tomatoes
1 cup beef stock
1 cup thinly sliced pepperoni
1/2 tsp dried basil
1 cup shredded mozzarella cheese

Directions:

In camp:
In saucepan, heat oil and stir fry onion, mushrooms and green pepper until soft but not browned. Add tomatoes, stock, pepperoni and basil. Cook until heated through. Ladle into bowls, sprinkle with cheese.

Leeky Kayak Potato Soup

Makes 4 servings

Ingredients:
2 tablespoons butter
2 leeks, trimmed and finely sliced
3 ½ cups chicken broth
3 - 4 medium size potatoes, chopped into cubes

Directions:

At home:
In a large saucepan, melt butter and sauté leeks for 10 minutes, or until soft. Add potato and broth. Increase heat and bring to boil, stirring then reduce heat and allow simmering for 5 minutes. Transfer to blender or food processor and puree until smooth. Return to pan and reheat until hot, but not boiling.

> Tips:
> Never bring food inside your tent, or use your stove inside or near your tent.

Mediterranean Chicken Stew

Makes 4 servings

Ingredients:
1 teaspoon cumin, ground
1 teaspoon coriander, ground
1 teaspoon paprika
¼ teaspoon ground ginger
1.5 kg chicken thighs, quartered
2 tablespoons olive oil
1 large onion, sliced
3 cloves garlic, minced
1 cup dry white wine
1 can crushed tomatoes
¼ cup chicken stock
2 teaspoons fresh oregano
¼ cup pitted black olives
¼ cup pitted green olives
3 tablespoons parsley, finely chopped

Directions:

At home:
In a small bowl, mix the cumin, coriander, paprika and ginger and then rub over chicken pieces. Heat oil in a large saucepan. Add chicken in batches and cook over medium heat until browned on all sides. Remove from pan. Reduce heat and add the onion stirring occasionally until browned. Add garlic and oregano and cook for 2 minutes. Add wine and cook an additional 5 minutes, or until nearly evaporated. Add the tomato, chicken stock and bring to boil. Return chicken to pan. Reduce heat and simmer, covered for 20 minutes. Stir in the olives and cook for 5 more minutes. Stir in the parsley.

Minty Cream of Pea Soup
(This one is a great light snack during a long paddle day)

Makes 2 servings

Ingredients:
½ cup skim milk
2 oz. peas
3 tablespoons whole-wheat flour
2 tablespoons dried chives
1 tablespoon dried mint
¼ teaspoon nutmeg
2 cloves garlic, minced
Salt and pepper to taste

Directions:

In camp:
In a medium cook pot, stir ingredients into 4 cups water. Bring to a boil, cover, reduce heat, and simmer for 5 minutes, stirring occasionally. Serve with bread or crackers.

More Rocko Stew

Makes 4 – 6 servings

Ingredients:
1 tablespoon vegetable stock powder
1 cup onion, chopped
2 cloves garlic, minced
1/3 cup olive oil
1 teaspoon dried thyme
¼ teaspoon ground cinnamon
½ teaspoon ginger, ground
¼ teaspoon nutmeg, ground
Pinch red chili flakes
1 cup sweet potato, diced
1 cup green beans, chopped
1 red bell pepper, seeded and chopped
1 can diced tomatoes
1/3 cup dried apricots, chopped
1 540 ml can black olives
3 tablespoons brown sugar
½ teaspoon turmeric
2 tablespoons lemon juice
Salt and pepper to taste
1/3 cup almonds, chopped
2 tablespoons dried parsley
2 cups couscous

Directions:

At home:
Make the couscous first. Boil 1 cup of water and pour in couscous. Allow to come to a quick boil, and then remove from heat and allow to steep, covered. Fluff with fork.
In a small saucepan bring 2 cups of water to a boil, add veggie stock and dissolve. Set aside. In a medium size pot, sauté onions and garlic in olive oil until the onions are translucent. Add spices, potatoes, green beans, bell pepper and tomatoes. Cook over high heat for five minutes. Add vegetable stock and apricots. Cover and let simmer on medium/low heat until veggies are tender. Stir in olives, brown sugar and simmer for about ten minutes. Add lemon juice and parsley, salt and pepper to taste. Serve on couscous and sprinkle almonds on top. Yum

> Tips:
> Cover your cook pots – contents will heat faster and the lids will keep out added ingredients such as leaves, twigs and bugs.

Pacific Rim Beef Stew

Makes 4 servings
Cooking time 1 – 2 hours

Ingredients:
2 tablespoons olive oil
1 chuck steak, cut into 1 inch cubes
1 large red onion, thickly sliced
3 cloves garlic, crushed
3 tablespoons tomato paste
1 cup red wine
2 cups beef stock
1 teaspoon fresh thyme, chopped
1 teaspoon fresh rosemary, chopped
3 tablespoons fresh coriander, chopped

Cooking:

At home:
In a large saucepan heat 1 tablespoon oil and add beef in batches over medium heat. Cook until browned. Remove from pan. Heat remaining oil, and add the onion, garlic and cook for 3 minutes. Add beef and onion/garlic mixture to crock pot. Stir in wine and remaining ingredients. Cook on low heat for one to two hours. Stir in 2 ½ tablespoons coriander and garnish with the remainder. Serve over rice.

Paddler Soup

Makes 4 servings
Cooking time in crock pot 2 – 6 hours

Ingredients:
1 12oz. can chicken broth
1 12oz. can V-8 juice
1/3 cup barley
1/3 cup pepperoni, ham or bacon, chopped
1 15oz. can cut green beans in liquid

Directions:

At home:
Place all ingredients in slow cooker, cover and cook on low for 2 to 6 hours.

Variations:
Try just about any veggie in this and it will work, diced potato, zucchini, some frozen corn. If the soup thickens up add a little more water before serving.

Spicy Sausage Stew

Makes 4 serving

Ingredients:
2 tablespoons olive oil
8 Italian sausages cut into 2cm lengths
1 leek, finely sliced
1 can diced tomatoes
½ cup chicken stock
1 can butter beans, rinsed and drained
1 1/3 cup couscous
8 oz. butter, melted
2 tablespoons fresh parsley

Directions:

At home:
Heat half the oil in a saucepan over medium heat and add sausage. Cook for 5 minutes or until browned. Remove and set aside. Cook the leek in the remaining oil over low heat for 10 minutes or until soft. Return sausage to pan and stir in tomato and stock. Bring to a boil. Then reduce heat and simmer for 30 minutes. Add beans and heat, stirring for 2 minutes. Cook couscous in pot with 1 1/3 cup boiling water and a pinch of salt. Let steep and fluff with fork. Divide couscous four ways and top with stew. Garnish with parsley.

Super Easy Chorizo and Beans

Makes 4 servings

Ingredients:
3 ½ cups vegetable stock
6 oz. chorizo, skinned and thickly sliced
1 can lima beans, drained
1 can tomatoes

Cooking:
At home, or in camp:
In a large saucepan, bring veggie stock to a boil. Add chorizo, stirring. Add beans, tomatoes and season to taste. Cover and simmer 15 – 20 minutes.

> Tips:
> Use a plastic funnel to fill the tank of your camping cook stove to avoid harmful spills.

Veggie Chili

Makes 6 servings

Ingredients:
3 tablespoons vegetable oil
2 large onions, chopped
3 cloves garlic, minced
2 green bell peppers, chopped
1 can diced tomatoes
4 small zucchinis, sliced 1 inch thick
2 cans chick peas (garbanzo), drained and rinsed
2 can kidney beans, drained and rinsed
1 tablespoon chili powder
1 tablespoon ground cumin
1 tablespoon dried basil
1 tablespoon dried oregano
1 teaspoon salt
1 teaspoon pepper
½ cup fresh parsley, chopped
¼ cup lemon juice
Directions:

At home:
In a medium saucepan, sauté onions, pepper, and garlic in oil over medium heat for 5 minutes. Add tomatoes and zucchini, cook uncovered for 30 minutes. Stir in chick peas and kidney beans, spices, herbs, parsley and lemon juice. Cook for 15 minutes.

(Variation, I also mix this in together with ½ cup cooked rice and use it for wraps.)

pastas:

Quick, filling and always satisfying while sitting in camp by the fire, pasta. With a few extra ingredients the base of the boring little pasta noodle can be turned into something very flavourful. Pasta is a 'go-to' for me on the first night of camping which is at the end of a long travel day to the kayaking destination.

Cheesey Beef

Makes 4 servings

Ingredients:
8 oz. Broad noodles
3l water
2 tablespoons vegetable oil
Salt and pepper to taste
1 sirloin steak, cut into ½ inch strips
2 cups sliced mushrooms
1 red pepper, cut into ¾ inch squares
½ teaspoon crushed chilies
2 tablespoons grated parmesan cheese

Directions:

In camp:
Cook pasta in boiling water according to package instructions. Drain, return to pot and keep warm. Heat oil in wok or frying pan on medium to high heat. Add beef and stir-fry to desired doneness. Sprinkle with salt and pepper to taste. Transfer to bowl. Heat remaining oil and add mushrooms, red pepper and chilies. Stir-fry for 2 – 3 minutes until tender crisp. Add beef to wok, and heat through. Add parmesan cheese, toss and pour over pasta. Sprinkle more parmesan cheese over top and serve hot.

Cold Pasta!

Some pastas are best served cold. On a good long paddle day, a container of pasta salad goes down easy as a satisfying snack and addition to lunch. These pasta dishes can be made ahead of time at home, packed in airtight containers and refrigerated.

Pasta Primavera with Herb Tomato Sauce

Makes 2 servings

Ingredients:
1 cup Rotini
1 cup broccoli florets
½ small zucchini, cut into ½-inch cubes
½ cup peas
1 small tomato cut into ½-inch cubes
1 tablespoon red bell pepper, seeded and chopped

For sauce:
1/3 cup water
2 tablespoons tomato paste
1 teaspoon olive oil
1 teaspoon red wine vinegar
½ teaspoon dried basil
½ teaspoon dried oregano
¼ teaspoon ground black pepper
¼ teaspoon garlic, minced

Directions:

At home:
To make sauce place all ingredients in a small bowl and mix well. Bring water to a boil in a medium size saucepan over medium to high heat, reduce heat and add rotini. Cook for about ten minutes or *al dente*. While pasta is cooking steam broccoli in veggie steamer for a bout 3 minutes or until tender but still crisp. When pasta is done, drain and rinse in cold water, drain again. In a medium size bowl toss together pasta, broccoli, zucchini, peas, cubed tomatoes and red pepper. Refrigerate until use.

Egg Noodles with Asparagus
(A great light dish for those hot summer evenings when no one wants to eat much)

Makes 2 servings

Ingredients:
250g egg noodles
½ bunch of asparagus (chopped)
1 large garlic clove (diced)
¼ cup olive oil
2 pinches of pepper
pinch of sea salt
¼ cup of parmesan cheese

Directions:

In camp:
Boil egg noodles, drain and set aside. Lightly steam the asparagus and chop into large chunks. In a large bowl mix together all of the ingredients. Serve as a side dish or a main meal.

Orzo in Lemon and Parmesan Cheese

Makes 4 servings

This one requires a bit of forethought but the garlic oil is worth the wait and good with other pastas as well. To make the garlic oil, place 6 cloves garlic, peeled and sliced in half together with 2 cups olive oil in a clean, sterilized bottle or jar with lid closed tightly for at least 3 weeks. Yep, three long weeks ahead of time. I am sure you could ask at your local grocer for this stuff but for me, and my paddling mates, half the fun is going the extra distance to make something from scratch. Bragging rights!

Ingredients:
10 oz. orzo pasta, roughly ½ - ¾ cup per person
5 tablespoons garlic oil
zest and juice of 2 lemons
1 cup Parmesan cheese, shredded

Directions:

In camp:
In a large pot, cook pasta according to package instructions, until tender. In a small bowl beat lemon zest with juice, and then add cheese and beat together until combined. Drain pasta and place in serving bowls, pour over the oil mixture and add lemon cheese mixture, toss to coat.

Penne with Tomato Pesto

Makes 2 servings

Ingredients: for tomato pesto
½ teaspoon olive oil
1 tablespoon onion, minced
¼ teaspoon garlic, minced
1 can tomatoes with juice
1 small tomato cut into ½ inch cubes
1 tablespoon sun-dried tomato, chopped
1 tablespoon parsley, minced
2 teaspoon fresh basil, minced
Ground black pepper to taste
Also will need 1 ½ cups penne pasta.

Directions:

In camp:
To make pesto, heat the olive oil in a medium saucepan over medium heat. Add onion; cook, stirring for one minute and add garlic; cook 30 seconds longer, stirring to prevent browning. Stir in canned tomatoes and juice. Quarter the tomatoes first. Stir in cubed tomatoes and pepper. Stir occasionally while heating over medium/low heat, uncovered for 10 minutes. Add parsley and basil. Cook pasta in boiling water over medium/high heat for ten minutes or until *al dente*.

When pasta is done, drain. Pour sauce over pasta and toss. Serve.

A cool variation is to toss in some sautéed chicken; about a ½ cup cubed boneless skinless chicken breast will do just fine.

curry:

Not everyone is as enthusiastic as I am about the taste of curry, but for me a curry is a great camping meal. It heats you up and goes well with a beer by the campfire or as you stare out upon the sea. The intensity of the flavour is entirely up to you, the camp cook. In some cases, less is definitely more, but I do like an extra half teaspoon of curry powder when cooking my recipes. I have added a few of my favorites in the Hungry Kayaker, give them a try and see what you think after eating curry in the great outdoors.

Chick Pea Curry

Makes 4 servings

Ingredients:
2 tablespoons vegetable oil
1 large onion, finely chopped
1 tablespoon curry powder
1 tablespoon flour
2 cups vegetable stock
½ cup raisins
¼ cup coconut milk
1 apple, peeled and grated
1 teaspoon tomato sauce
1 teaspoon sugar
1 teaspoon Worcestershire sauce
1 can chick peas, drained and rinsed
1 ½ cups cooked rice

Directions:

In camp:
In a fry pan, sauté onion in oil over medium heat until tender. Stir in curry powder and flour. Gradually add stock, stirring constantly. Add all other ingredients, except chick peas and rice. Let simmer for 15 minutes. Add chick peas, and heat through for about 5 minutes. Serve over cooked rice. A little chutney on the side is tasty with some flat bread!

Clayoquot Curry

Makes 2 servings

Ingredients:
¼ cup tomato sauce
5 teaspoons curry powder
1 tablespoon parsley flakes
½ teaspoon cumin
½ teaspoon coriander
½ teaspoon ground ginger
½ teaspoon tarragon
1 onion, chopped
2 cloves garlic, minced
2 teaspoon tamari soy sauce
1 can shrimp, drained, or the seafood of your choice

Directions:

At home:
Measure all dry ingredients into a Ziploc bag.

In camp:
In a medium saucepan, sauté onion in oil and stir in remaining ingredients (except seafood) when onion is softened. Stir in 2 cups of water and bring mixture to a boil. Reduce heat, cover and simmer 5 – 10 minutes. Add seafood, heat and serve

Curried Chicken Pita

Makes 4 servings

Ingredients:
1 cup cooked chicken, diced
½ apple, finely chopped
¼ cup raisins
1 stalk celery, finely chopped
1 green onion, thinly sliced
2 tablespoons mayonnaise
2 tablespoons yogurt
1 teaspoon curry powder
1 teaspoon salt
1 teaspoon pepper
½ cup lettuce chopped
4 whole-wheat pitas, cut in half to form pockets

Directions:
In camp:
In a medium bowl, combine chicken, apple, raisins, celery and onion. Combine mayonnaise, yogurt, curry powder, salt and pepper. Stir into chicken mixture. Place a layer of lettuce at bottom of pita pocket followed by a spoonful of chicken mixture, add more lettuce on top.

A couple tablespoons of mango chutney to the chicken mixture is very good as a variation.

Curried Thai Noodlies

Makes 4 servings

Ingredients:
4 packages instant noodles
1 large sweet onion, sliced
2 cloves garlic, minced
1 red bell pepper, seeded and slivered
1 yellow bell pepper, seeded and slivered
1 can unsweetened coconut milk
1 teaspoon sesame oil
3 tablespoons olive oil
Sweet thai chili sauce
Handful of snap peas
1/3 cup chopped dried apricots
1/3 cup slivered almonds
1/3 cup cashews, chopped
½ cup unsweetened coconut, shredded
¼ cup currants
2 tablespoons brown sugar
2 tablespoons curry powder
½ teaspoon cinnamon

Directions:

At home:
Mix into a large Ziploc bag the nuts, dried fruit, coconut, brown sugar and spices.

In camp:
Bring some water to a boil to soften noodles in a small pot. In a wok, heat olive and sesame oil, sauté onions over medium heat until soft. Add red and yellow peppers and sauté a few more minutes. Add pre-mix of dried ingredients, sauté and mix well. Add coconut milk. Reduce heat and let simmer until apricots and currants are soft. Add chili sauce to taste, mix well and serve on top of noodles.

Green Chicken Curry
(a personal favorite, but tough to find green chickens)

Makes 4 servings

Ingredients:
(below is a list of ingredients to make green curry paste, but a faster solution during the pre-trip shopping is to pick up a small jar of green curry paste.)
4 fresh green chilies, chopped
1 small onion, chopped
4 cloves garlic, chopped
1 cup fresh coriander
2 tablespoons oil
1 teaspoon coriander seeds
½ teaspoon cumin seeds
400ml coconut milk
2 boneless, skinless chicken breasts, cut into cubes
2 tablespoons sugar
1 tablespoon lime juice
3 tablespoons fresh basil, chopped
4 – 6 medium mushrooms, sliced

Directions:

At home:
Place chili, onion, garlic, coriander, and oil into blender and process to a smooth paste. Add coriander seeds, cumin seeds, and blend to combine. Place paste from blender into a container or Ziploc bag.

In camp:
In a frying pan place, curry paste and cook, stirring over medium heat for 2 minutes. Add half the coconut milk and cook, stirring for 5 minutes. Add chicken and mushrooms. Stir in remaining coconut milk and simmer for 10 minutes or until chicken is cooked. Stir in fish sauce, sugar, lime-juice and basil. Serve in bowls over rice.

Race Rocks Rice Curry

Makes 2 servings

Ingredients:
1 cup short-grain rice
2 tablespoons onion, chopped finely
2 ½ teaspoons curry powder, or more to taste
½ teaspoon salt
2 tablespoons almonds, slivered
2 tablespoons cashews
¼ cup raisins
6 dried apricot halves, cut into bits
6 dried apple rings, cut into bits
¼ cup unsweetened coconut, shredded
3 cups water

Directions:

At home:
Measure rice into Ziploc bag and separately bag curry powder and salt. Another bag will contain fruits, nuts and another for the coconut.

In camp:
Bring 3 cups of water to a boil in a large saucepan over medium heat. Stir in rice, onion, curry powder and salt. Cover and simmer on low heat for 15 minutes. Stir in nuts and fruit, cover and simmer an additional 5 minutes. Serve with coconut sprinkled on top.

Thai Shrimp

Makes 4 servings

Ingredients:
1 can coconut milk
1 teaspoon Thai curry paste, red
1/3 cup water
1 tablespoon brown sugar
1 tablespoon soy sauce
1 pound raw shrimp, peeled
½ cup fresh basil leaves, thinly sliced
1 cup cooked jasmine rice, or rice vermicelli

Directions:

In camp:
In a pot, cook rice in 2 cups water for 15 minutes. Fluff with fork when done.

Pour half the coconut milk into a saucepan an bring to a boil over medium heat, stirring occasionally. Cook for 5 minutes; oils may start to surface but that is okay. Stir in curry paste and cook for about 2 minutes more.

Stir together remaining milk and water. Add to pan with brown sugar and soy sauce. Cook over medium/high heat for 10 minutes or until sauce thickens slightly.

Add shrimp and basil, reduce heat to low. Cook 3 minutes or until shrimp turn pink. Serve over rice.

Tidal Rapids Rice Curry, oh my!

Makes 2 servings

Ingredients:
1 cup basmati rice, or quinoa (a tasty grain)
1 onion, chopped
2 teaspoons curry powder
½ teaspoon salt
A handful of each dried fruit, chopped; Raisins, dates, apricots
A handful of almonds and cashews, chopped

Directions:

At home:
Measure dried fruit and nuts into separate Ziploc bags. The rice, and or quinoa can also be pre-packaged for convenience.

In camp:
In a medium saucepan, bring 3 cups water to a boil, stir in all ingredients. Return to a boil, cover, and reduce heat to medium/low and simmer 15 – 20 minutes. Stir frequently to prevent scorching.

stir-fries!

If serving with rice, bring rice and 2 cups water to a boil, reduce heat to low and simmer for 15 minutes using a pot riser to prevent scorching. I will often start the rice to a boil and after a few minutes of simmer will set it aside covered and the pot wrapped in a towel to steep. I have had lots of success with unburned rice on the bottom of the pot, not to mention fluffier rice using this method. In addition, it frees up your single-burner stove to cook the rest of the meal.

3 B's Stir Fry
Beef, Bok Choy, and Basil

Makes 4 servings

Ingredients:
1lb. beef stir-fry strips, or sirloin steak
6 baby bok choy
6 green onion
1 large red bell pepper
3 cloves garlic
½ cup teriyaki sauce, or soy sauce
1tbsp cornstarch
¼ cup red wine
1 tbsp liquid honey
1-1 ½ tsp dried basil
1tbsp veggie oil

Directions:

At home:
If using sirloin steaks then cut into thin strips and place into a Ziploc bag. If using pre-cut stir-fry beef then place into a sealed Ziploc bag.
  Mince garlic finely. In a small bowl stir teriyaki sauce with cornstarch until dissolved. Stir in garlic, wine, honey and dried basil. Mix well and pour into a sealed container or Ziploc bag.
  Wash bok choy. Slice leaves and stalks crosswise into 1 inch strips. Put into a separate Ziploc to the red bell pepper which will be cut into strips. (Or take the whole pepper to camp and cut it into thin strips there).

In camp:
Thinly slice green onion and bell peppers if you are choosing to do that in camp, and set aside.

Heat oil in wok or fry pan over medium/high heat. Add beef strips and stir-fry until lightly browned. Stir in bok choy and cook until wilted. Add bell pepper.

Stir in teriyaki mixture remembering first to give it a good stir in its container. Reduce heat to medium and cook, stirring often until sauce has thickened.

Stir in green onion and serve immediately over wild rice.

> Tips:
> Did you know that temperature affects your appetite?

Asparagus Mushroom Stir-Fry

Makes 4 servings

Ingredients:
½ lb. asparagus
2 tablespoons olive oil
2 shallots, thinly sliced
½ cup shiitake mushrooms, sliced stemmed caps
¼ teaspoon salt
¼ teaspoon ground black pepper
½ cup chicken stock
1 cup uncooked jasmine rice

Directions:

In camp:
Cook rice according to package, set aside and fluff with fork.

Trim off tough ends of asparagus, cut stalks diagonally into 4 pieces. In a saucepan of boiling water, blanch asparagus until tender crisp and drain well.

In a wok, heat oil over medium/high heat. Stir-fry shallots until softened, but not browned. Add asparagus, mushrooms, salt, pepper and stir-fry mushrooms until wilted and asparagus is tender.

Add chicken stock and cook, stirring often until no liquid remains.

Serve over or with rice.

Beef Noodles

Makes 4 servings

Ingredients:
300g (about 1/3 package) linguine, uncooked
3 cups broccoli florets
2 cups carrots, sliced
2 teaspoons vegetable oil
1 sirloin steak, cut into thin strips
3 baby bok choy, cut into strips about 1 inch
1 large red bell pepper, sliced thinly
¼ cup teriyaki sauce
1 teaspoon ground ginger

Directions:

At home:
Cut carrots, and broccoli and place in Ziploc bag. Wash and cut bok choy into 1 inch strips, then place into separate bag. Cut steak into strips and bag. The bell pepper you can cut now, or carry whole into camp and cut it fresh there.

In camp:
In a large pot, cook pasta according to package instructions, adding carrots and broccoli to the water for the last couple of minutes of pasta cooking time. Set aside just before noodles are fully cooked and allow to steep in pot.

Heat oil in wok or large fry pan. Add meat and cook until browned, stirring occasionally. Stir in teriyaki sauce and ginger; cook until sauce thickens, stirring occasionally.

Place pasta mixture into serving bowl. Add meat mixture and toss lightly.

Chicken Noodle Stir-Fry

Makes 4 servings

Ingredients:
6 boneless skinless chicken thighs
1 tablespoon soy sauce
1 tablespoon sesame oil
¼ teaspoon ground black pepper
2 cloves garlic, minced
1 lb. baby bok choy
2 tablespoons vegetable oil
1 teaspoon ginger, minced
1 sweet red pepper, thinly sliced
2 packs dried 'ramen' noodles
1 green onion, thinly sliced
Directions:

Cut chicken into cubes. In a bowl, toss together chicken, soy sauce, sesame oil, pepper and half the garlic. Marinate for ten minutes. Cut bok choy in half lengthwise and set aside.

In a wok, heat 1 tablespoon of vegetable oil over high heat. Stir-fry chicken until browned. Add bok choy, red pepper, ginger, and remaining garlic. Stir-fry until veggies are tender crisp and transfer to plate.

Add 1-cup water and remaining vegetable oil to wok and bring to a boil. Add noodles to wok, cover steam until softened and loose. Break noodles apart with spoon and return chicken mixture to wok. Stir until heated.

Chicken, Snow Peas and Cashews Stir-Fry

Makes 4 servings

Ingredients:
3 tablespoons soy sauce
4 teaspoons corn starch
1 tablespoon sugar
1 tablespoon chicken stock
1 teaspoon sesame oil
Dash hot pepper sauce
2 boneless skinless chicken breasts, cut into cubes
1 cup snow peas, strings removed and cut diagonally in half
1 bell pepper, sliced into bite-sized pieces
1 tablespoon vegetable oil
1/3 cup roasted cashews
1 clove garlic, sliced
1 1/2 tablespoon ginger, sliced

Directions:

At home:
Pre-cook chicken if so desired and put in a Ziploc bag until needed.

In camp:
In a bowl, mix together soy sauce, cornstarch, sugar, chicken stock, sesame oil, and hot pepper sauce; set aside.

In a wok heat vegetable oil over high heat, stir-fry chicken in batches until browned; transfer to plate.

Add snow peas, bell pepper, cashews, garlic and ginger to wok. Cover and steam until peppers are tender crisp.

Return chicken to wok along with any juices; combine. Stir in soy sauce mixture and simmer until glossy.

> Tips:
> Did you know there are about 100,000 bacteria in every litre of drinking water?

Lemon Ginger Chicken Stir-Fry

Makes 4 servings

Ingredients:
1 teaspoon grated lemon rind
1/3 cup lemon juice
1 small fresh red chili, chopped finely
1 clove garlic, crushed
1 tablespoon grated ginger
2 tablespoons fresh coriander, chopped
2 boneless, skinless chicken breasts, sliced
1 tablespoon sesame seeds
2 tablespoons oil
Handful of snow peas, halved lengthwise
Handful baby corn, quartered
2 tablespoons soy sauce

Directions:

At home:
Place lemon rind, juice, chili, garlic, ginger and coriander in a large bowl and mix. Add chicken, mix to coat and marinate in refrigerator. Place in large Ziploc bag, removing air and seal. Put in freezer.

In camp:
Heat a wok over high heat and sesame seeds and stir-fry for 30 seconds. Remove from pan. Heat 1-tablespoon oil and add chicken from bag. Stir-fry in batches until lightly browned on all sides. Remove and set aside.
Heat the remaining oil and add snow peas, baby corn and soy sauce. Stir-fry for 2 minutes. Return chicken to wok, stir-fry for about a minute or so. Sprinkle sesame seeds over top and serve with rice or noodles.

Spicy Thai Beef and Noodles

Makes 2 servings

Ingredients:
3 oz rice noodles
2 tablespoons vegetable oil
2 cloves garlic, minced
1 jalapeño pepper, seeded and sliced
1 grilling steak, thinly sliced
2 tablespoons soy sauce
1 cup green beans, chopped
2 teaspoons lime juice
2/3 cup bean sprouts
¼ cup coriander, chopped
2 tablespoons parsley, chopped

Directions:

In camp:
In a large bowl, cover noodles with boiling water and let stand 15 minutes.

In a wok, heat oil over high heat and stir-fry garlic and jalapeno pepper for 30 seconds. Add beef and stir-fry until browned but pink inside. Transfer to plate.

Add beans, 2 tablespoons water, soy sauce, lime juice and sugar to wok. Cover and cook until beans are tender crisp. Add noodles and stir-fry until tender. Return beef to wok and sprouts and toss to combine well and heat through. Add parsley and coriander and toss to combine.

Stir-Fried Beef and Rice

Makes 4 servings

Ingredients:
1 cup cooked rice
1 cup snow peas, sliced
2 carrots, thinly sliced
1 tablespoon vegetable oil
12 oz grilling steak, cut into thin strips
1 clove garlic, minced
1 teaspoon ginger, minced
2 tablespoon soy sauce
¼ teaspoon ground black pepper
¼ teaspoon hot pepper sauce
1 cup bean sprouts
2 green onions, thinly sliced

Directions:

In camp:
In a saucepan bring 2 to 3 cups water to a boil and add rice. Cover and reduce heat and allow simmering for 15 minutes.
Add snap peas and carrots, cook covered until vegetables are tender crisp and no liquid remains. Fluff with fork.

Meanwhile, in a wok heat half the oil over medium/high heat. Stir-fry beef, garlic and ginger until beef is browned but pink inside. Transfer to a bowl. Add soy sauce, 2 tablespoons water, pepper and hot pepper sauce to beef. Toss to coat.

Add remaining oil to wok and stir-fry rice mixture for 2 minutes then add beef mixture. Stir-fry until heated through.
Stir in bean sprouts and green onions.

> Tips:
> Did you know that over half the world's population live on a staple diet of rice?

rice:

Rice is an excellent ingredient to carry in your kayak kitchen bag. As part of a recipe, or as a wholesome and nutritional bed for your meal to be poured over rice is indeed nice, In addition, if combined with beef, it creates a very easy to metabolize protein which will refresh and restore your body at the end of the day.

Creamy Asparagus Risotto

Makes 4 servings

Ingredients:
2 tablespoons olive oil
1 medium onion, finely chopped
1 cups rice, uncooked
1 cup asparagus, cut into in inch pieces
2 cups chicken stock
2 tablespoons cream cheese
¼ cup lemon juice

Directions:

In camp:
In wok heat oil over medium heat, add onion and cook, stirring occasionally for 2 minutes or until tender. Stir in rice, and broth. Bring to a boil, reduce heat and simmer for 15 minutes adding asparagus after about 10 minutes. Add cream cheese and juice, fluffing with a fork until blended.

Creamy Rice, Spinach and Chicken

Makes 4 servings

Ingredients:
2 boneless skinless chicken breasts, cut into strips
1 cup chicken stock
1 cup jasmine rice, uncooked
6 cups torn baby spinach leaves
1 tomato, chopped
2 tablespoons parmesan cheese, finely grated
2 tablespoons oil
¼ cup cream cheese, cut into cubes
Directions:
In camp:

In a pot, heat oil and add chicken; cook until lightly browned on all sides. Add chicken stock and bring to a boil. Stir in rice and again bring to a boil. Reduce heat, cover and simmer for 15 minutes.

When rice is nearly cooked add cream cheese and stir until melted completely. Add spinach and cover, cooking until leaves are wilted. Remove from heat. Stir in tomato and sprinkle with parmesan cheese.

Grilled Chicken and Asparagus Risotto

Makes 2 servings

Ingredients: for asparagus risotto
1 small onion, finely chopped
1 cup jasmine rice, uncooked
2 cups chicken stock
½ lb. asparagus, cut into 1-inch pieces
1 ½ tablespoons light cream cheese

Ingredients: for chicken
2 boneless skinless chicken breasts
¼ cup lime juice
1 tablespoon garlic, crushed
1 teaspoon chili powder
Pinch ground black pepper

Cooking:

At home
In a bowl, mix together lime juice, garlic, chili powder and pepper. Rinse chicken breasts under cold water and let marinate in mixture for one hour in the refrigerator. Pack in Ziploc and keep cool. Freezing the chicken is a good idea and in a cooler bag will double as an icepack for other fresh ingredients.

In camp:
In a cook pot, bring rice and chicken stock to a boil, reduce heat and simmer for 15 minutes. Adding asparagus in the last few minutes. When cooked fluff with fork. Meanwhile, assuming you have a good cooking campfire on the go, place chicken breasts over coals and cook about 10 minutes per side or until juices run clear.
When rice is cooked blend in cream cheese until completely mixed in. Serve as side dish to chicken.

Hatch Cover Sushi

Makes 8 pieces

Ingredients:
½ cup uncooked sushi rice
1 ½ cups water
1 teaspoon wasabi powder, or paste
Three 5 by ¼ inch strips cucumber
Six 2 by ¼ inch avocado strips
Two 5 by ¼ inch strips imitation crab meat
One 8-inch sheet dried seaweed, (hoshi nori)

Special equipment: Bamboo mat (sudare) found at any grocery store in the Asian foods section.. Also for accompaniments, soy sauce and pickled ginger.

Directions:

In camp:
In a saucepan bring rice and water to a boil, reduce heat and allow to simmer for 10 minutes. Remove pan from heat and allow steaming for 5 more minutes.

Unless you have a tube of wasabi paste, place wasabi powder in a small bowl and with a teaspoon of water stir into a paste. While rice is cooking, prepare filling ingredients and set aside. When rice is cooked set it aside uncovered to cool to room temperature. Being careful not to burn your fingers wave the seaweed sheet over your stove flame for about 15 seconds, then flip the sheet and repeat.

To assemble the rolls...

1). Place the sheet of seaweed rough side up with the longer edge facing you. Spread rice over surface in a even layer. This is done on the bamboo mat, (you can substitute this mat with plastic wrap).

2). Flip, placing the seaweed side up, rice down. Spread a small amount of the wasabi paste down the center of the sheet. Then place strips of crab meat, cucumber and avacado down the center from edge to edge.

3). With the mat attached roll up by hand, squeezing firmly as you roll. Press down on all four sides to form a square tube.

4). Remove mat or wrap and place on cutting board (hatch covers will do) and with a wet knife (serrated is best) cut the roll in half with a sawing motion. Moisten the knife between cuts, this is very important as the seaweed might tear otherwise. Now cut each half section into four more.

Eat by hand, serve with soy sauce for dipping and a small amount of wasabi. Add pickled ginger between bites for enhanced flavours.

Pacific Rim Lentils and Rice

Makes 2 servings

Ingredients:
½ cup basmati rice
½ cup lentils
2 tablespoons butter
1 medium onion, chopped
½ teaspoon salt
½ teaspoon cinnamon
½ teaspoon ginger
½ teaspoon cardamom
1 bay leaf
Pinch of cayenne

Directions:

In camp:
In a medium cook pot bring 2 ½ cups of water to a boil and stir in mixture. Return to a boil, cover and reduce heat allowing to simmer for 15 – 20 minutes, stirring occasionally. Remove bay leaf and serve.

(variations: use quinoa instead of rice.)

Zucchini Risotto

Makes 4 servings

Ingredients:
1 litre chicken or vegetable stock
2 tablespoons olive oil
1 onion, finely chopped
1 2/3 cup Arborio rice
1/3 cup dry sherry
3 teaspoons grated lemon rind
2 tablespoons lemon juice
1½ cup zucchini, diced
2 tablespoons fresh parsley, chopped
½ cup grated Parmesan cheese

Directions:

In camp:
In a large pot bring stock to a boil, and then reduce heat and simmer, covered on low heat. In a saucepan heat the oil and add the onion, cooking for 5 minutes on medium heat. Reduce heat and add ½-cup hot stock and rice, stirring constantly. Gradually add stock ½ cup at a time and cook 20 minutes, stirring constantly. If risotto becomes too dry add more stock or water. Stir in sherry, lemon rind, lemon juice, and zucchini. Cook over low heat for 5 minutes, or until risotto is tender. Stir in parsley and half the parmesan cheese. Garnish with rest of parmesan.

camp fire grilling:

Okay, so if your have read the section on campfires you will know that I tend to like a bit of grilling now and then. Which is to say just about every kayaking trip. There is, and I say this very confidently, nothing better than the taste of anything grilled on a campfire as the sunsets and the beer is cold close at hand. You will need a good grilling fire of course. I will often get the campfire going and let it burn down to the point that the embers are glowing and have that rolling rippling heated appearance. There is immense heat from them and it is even heat good for cooking. After you have finished cooking add some small bits of wood to the coals and you will be up and running with a comfortable evening campfire again. A metal grill top that fits your small fire pit is a good bit of kit to bring with you on a trip. On an early expedition, as a last minute substitute for a proper grill we picked up a set of cooling racks for baking. They worked fine and eliminated the usual balancing act of kabob skewers. Ash and dirt is not a great added ingredient.

Beef Kabobies

Makes 1 – 2 kabobs

Ingredients:
For sauce:
1 cup olive oil
¾ cup soy sauce
¼ cup Worcestershire sauce
2 tablespoons mustard
½ teaspoon ground black pepper
½ teaspoon salt
½ cup red wine vinegar
1 teaspoon dried parsley
2 cloves garlic, crushed
¼ cup lemon juice

For kabobs:
1 top sirloin steak cut into 1 inch squares
Cherry tomatoes, pint
½ red bell pepper, cut into 1 inch pieces
4 – 8 mushrooms

Directions:

At home:
Mix all marinade ingredients together in a small bowl. Pour into a large Ziploc bag and add meat. Making sure all the beef is coated in sauce. Seal bag and refrigerate.

In camp:
Thread beef, tomatoes, peppers and mushrooms onto skewers. Grill, turning occasionally for 7 – 10 minutes per side or until cooked through. Serve.

> Tips:
> Keep your first aid kit well-stocked with fresh bandages and supplies. Keep it in a water-tight durable container.

Chicken Kabobies in Tomato

Makes 1 – 2 kabobs

Ingredients:
 For sauce:
1 tablespoon soy sauce
1 teaspoon honey
1 teaspoon tomato paste
¼ teaspoon garlic, minced
Dash of ground black pepper, or to taste

For kabobs:
½ boneless, skinless chicken breast cut into 1-inch squares
¼ cup pineapple chunks
6 ¼ inch slices zucchini

Directions:

At home:
Mix marinade ingredients in a small bowl, mix well with a whisk or fork and pour into a large Ziploc bag, add chicken chunks and seal bag. Refrigerate and keep cold in a cooler bag in your kayak until use.
In camp:
Thread alternately the chicken, pineapple and zucchini onto skewers. This recipe should get you three good ones. Grill over coals until chicken is cooked through, turning occasionally. Serve on a plate with rice or couscous.

Lamb Kabobies (Spicy)

Makes 1 -2 kabobs

Ingredients:
For sauce:
2 tablespoons lemon juice
½ cup olive oil
1 teaspoon garlic, minced
½ teaspoon cumin

For kabobs:
4 oz lamb, cut into 1-inch squares
6 ¼ inch slices zucchini
½ 1 red bell pepper, cut into 1-inch pieces
6 – 10 mushrooms

Directions:

At home:
Mix all marinade ingredients in a small bowl, mix well and pour into a large Ziploc bag. Add lamb to marinade, making sure all the meat is coated, seal bag and refrigerate.

In camp:
Thread alternately the lamb, pepper, zucchini, and mushrooms. Grill for 5 – 7 minutes per side or until cooked through. Serve with rice or couscous. Try a bit of hummus for dipping.

Lamb Kabobies…(that are a little tamer)

Makes 1 -2 kabobs

Ingredients:
 For sauce:
1 clove garlic, minced
1 cup onion, chopped
¼ cup apple cider vinegar
¼ cup olive oil

For kabobs:
4 oz. lamb cut into 1-inch squares
6 ¼ inch slices zucchini
4 – 10 mushrooms
Cherry tomatoes, pint

Directions:

At home:
Combine all ingredients for marinade in a small bowl, mix well and pour into a large Ziploc bag. Add lamb to marinade and seal the bag, making sure all the meats is coated. Refrigerate.

In camp:
Alternately, threat lamb, zucchini, mushrooms and tomatoes, and grill for 5 – 7 minutes per side or until cooked through. Serve with rice, or couscous.

Spicy Beef Kabobies

Makes 1 – 2 kabobs

Ingredients:
 For sauce:
2 cloves garlic, minced
2 teaspoons paprika
½ teaspoon turmeric
1 teaspoon cumin
1 teaspoon salt
½ teaspoon ground black pepper
½ cup red wine vinegar
¼ cup olive oil

For kabobs:
1 top sirloin steak, cut into 1-inch squares
6 ¼ inch slices zucchini
Cherry tomatoes, pint
½ red bell pepper, cut into 1-inch pieces
6 – 8 mushrooms

Directions:

At home:
Combine all ingredients for marinade, pour into a large Ziploc bag and add meat. Seal bag and refrigerate.

In camp:
Thread alternating beef, zucchini, tomatoes, peppers and mushrooms. Grill 7 – 10 minutes per side, turning occasionally until cooked through. Serve.

assorted dinner ideas:

When compiling the list of recipes I wanted to include in the Hungry Kayaker there were some, old favorites of mine that just did not manage to fit correctly under any specific category. The left overs! Here a few delicious ideas.

Baby Seal Cakes

Makes about a dozen squares

Ingredients:
6 cups shredded baby seal, (substitute with 10 carrots, shredded if seal is not plentiful in your area.)
1 small onion, chopped
2 cloves garlic, crushed
¼ cup whole-wheat flour
½ cup whole-wheat bread crumbs
2 eggs, beaten
1 cup grated Parmesan cheese
Dash of ground black pepper
Pinch of ground nutmeg

Directions:

At Home:
Combine ingredients in a bowl and mix well. Spread into a greased or non-stick 12x18 pan and cover with foil. Bake at 350 degrees for 45 minutes. Remove foil and bake for another 15 minutes. Let cool, but cut into squares while still warm. When cold removed squares from pan, and then wrap them individually in wax paper and put into large Ziploc bag or plastic container.

Beer Battered Oysters in Jalapeno Sauce

Ingredients:
For Oysters:
Veggie oil for frying, enough to fill a medium cook pot with a bout 2 inches
1 cup all-purpose flour
1 cup cornstarch
2 teaspoons salt
½ teaspoon baking powder
11 oz. cold beer (lagar)
Tabasco sauce, to taste
15 large shucked oysters

For sauce:
½ cup mayonnaise
1 tablespoon capers, chopped
½ teaspoon Dijon mustard
1 teaspoon lemon juice
4 – 10 pickled jalapeno peppers. (4 for flavour, and up to 10 for levels of killer spicey)
1 tablespoon parsley, chopped
2 tablespoons onion, finely chopped

Directions:
Heat oil in cook pot on high. While oil is heating mix in a large bowl the flour, cornstarch, salt and baking powder. Make the sauce as well (this can be made ahead of time at home, and kept refrigerated). To make sauce, whisk ingredients in a small bowl.

When oil is ready add the beer to the dry ingredients in the large bowl. Stir until the bubbling slows down and season to taste with Tabasco. Stir again to blend it all together.

Dip 2 oysters at a time into the beer batter and coat completely. Carefully drop them into the hot oil. A slotted spoon is a very handy thing to have for this recipe. Do six oysters per batch, frying them for one to two minutes each and lifting them with a slotted spoon to a plate covered in paper towel. Allow the oil to reheat between batches. Serve hot with a nice cold beer at hand.

> Tips:
> Read! Bring along a good book for that time in camp or if the weather gets rainy, the best time is 'tent time'!

Chicken Chimichangas

Makes 4 servings

Ingredients:
2 boneless skinless chicken breasts
¼ cup vegetable oil
1 onion, chopped
1 jalapeno pepper, diced, seeds removed
1 teaspoon oregano
1 cup cooked rice (leftovers can be used for lunch the next day in wraps)
2 roma tomatoes, diced
1 cup Monterey Jack cheese, grated
4 whole-wheat tortillas
salt and pepper to taste
Handful of toothpicks (Snip off the ends of the wooden grilling skewers for this)

Directions:

At home:
Precook chicken by placing chicken breasts in water and bring to a boil. Reduce heat and simmer for 15 - 20 minutes until cooked through. Allow chicken to cool slightly and shred into small pieces. Put chicken into a Ziploc bag and refrigerate until needed.

In camp:
In a pot, cook rice. When done fluff with fork and set aside.
In a pot, heat a tablespoon of oil and sauté onion, pepper and oregano. Add shredded chicken and fry for 5 minutes. Stir in cooked rice, tomatoes, and fry until the rice has absorbed most of the liquid. Set aside to cool slightly and mix in cheese.
Preparing the Chimichanga is done by placing filling in the middle of the tortilla. Roll the tortilla into a fat tube shape and then fold the ends towards the middle and hold in place with toothpicks. Heat about ¼ cup oil in a fry pan and fry up the Chimichangas until golden brown on both sides. Serve with salsa.

> Tips:
> Go online and check out the areas you want to explore by kayak. It is always good to get a head's up on things to better prepare for your adventures.

Chicken Satay over Couscous

Makes 2 servings

Ingredients:
For sauce:
4 tablespoons peanut butter
2 tablespoons sesame oil
1 tablespoon soy sauce
1 tablespoon honey
1 tablespoon coconut milk
1 clove garlic, crushed
½ lime, juice only

For chicken:
2 boneless, skinless chicken breasts cut into strips
1 onion, sliced thinly
¼ cup red bell pepper, chopped finely
1 teaspoon oil
1 teaspoon garlic, crushed
½ cup couscous

Directions:

At home:
Precook chicken strips until pink is gone and place in Ziploc bag.

In camp:
Cook couscous first and set aside in covered dish. To cook couscous, add 1 cup water and couscous in a small saucepan. Bring to boil and set aside. This takes very little time to cook so pay attention. No one like crusty couscous. Fluff with fork.

Over medium to high heat, heat oil in wok. Stir-fry chicken in small batches until browned all over, and set aside in covered dish or bowl.
Place onion and garlic in wok; stir-fry until onion softens, add chicken back into wok with remaining ingredients and 1/3 cup satay sauce. Stir contents of wok until sauce thickens slightly. Serve over couscous.

Gloop! an old family recipe

Makes 2 servings

Ingredients:
1 can cream of mushroom soup
1 tablespoon vegetable oil
½ cup frozen peas
½ cup broccoli florets
½ cup carrots, grated
¼ cup mushrooms, chopped
1 cup uncooked jasmine rice
1 teaspoon ground black pepper
1 teaspoon chili powder
1 clove garlic, sliced
1 small onion, finely chopped

Directions:

In camp:
In a large cook pot bring rice and 2 cups water to a boil, reduce heat and simmer until cooked. Add carrots and broccoli in last couple minutes of cooking. Remove from heat and fluff with fork.

Meanwhile, in a small saucepan, heat oil and add garlic and onion. Sauté until onion is cooked, but not browned. Add mushroom soup with half a can of water, stir until blended. Simmer for five minutes and then add mushrooms and seasonings. Simmer on low heat. When rice is cooked, add the sauce mixture to the rice, and blend. Serve while hot.

Grilled Scallops

Makes 4 Servings

Ingredients:

16 scallops, frozen and shelled
1 bunch sage leaves
3 tablespoons olive oil
1 tablespoon balsamic vinegar

Directions:

In camp:
Dry scallops in paper towel. Heat fry pan over high heat and cook scallops in each side for 2 – 3 minutes. Add sage leaves and cook until wilting. Beat together oil and vinegar in a bowl. Remove scallops from heat and toss well with vinegar dressing. Season to taste. Serve.

Lamb and Zucchini

Makes 2 servings

Ingredients:

2 lamb chops
1 can diced tomatoes
1 cup zucchini, sliced
¼ cup sliced mushrooms
3 tablespoons basil, chopped

Directions:

In camp:
In a large saucepan, brown chops on both sides over medium to high heat. Reduce heat to medium and add tomato, mushrooms, and zucchini. Cover and simmer 20 – 30 minutes using a heat diffuser to stop any scorching. Cook until meat is tender and then stir in basil and cook a couple more minutes. Serve with rice.

Orange Ginger Chicken and Broccoli

Makes 2 servings

Ingredients:
For sauce:
½ cup orange juice
2 tablespoons soy sauce
1 teaspoon sesame oil
1 teaspoon brown sugar
¼ teaspoon chili paste
1 clove garlic, minced
1 slice ginger, minced
Oil for stir fry, as needed
Also will need:
2 boneless, skinless chicken breasts cut into 1 inch cubes. Substitute chicken for sirloin beef cut into strips.
1 cup broccoli florets

Directions:

At home:
Cut chicken into strips and cook until pink is gone then when cool cut into cubes and place into Ziploc bag.

In camp:
Combine all sauce ingredients in a measuring cup, except garlic and ginger.
In a wok heat oil, then add garlic and ginger. Stir-fry until aromatic. Add chicken and cook until browned, add broccoli and stir-fry until tender. Push ingredients up the sides of the wok and pour in the sauce, slowly stir together and cook for about 5 minutes more. Serve over couscous or rice.

Salmon in Tomato and Orange Sauce

Makes 2 servings

Ingredients:
¼ cup tomato sauce
3 tablespoons whole-wheat flour
1 onion, chopped
¼ cup mushrooms, finely chopped
2 cloves garlic, crushed
1 teaspoon grated orange rind
½ teaspoon salt
4 – 6 sun-dried tomatoes, chopped
Pinch of cayenne
1 can salmon, drained

Directions:

In camp:
Place ingredients in medium size sauce pan and stir in 2 ½ cups water. Bring mixture to a boil over medium/high heat, stirring constantly to prevent scorching. Reduce heat, cover and simmer for 5 minutes.
Serve over rice or pasta.

Sweet and Sour Lentils

Makes 2 – 4 servings

Ingredients:
2 cups water
2 teaspoons vegetable stock powder
1 cup dried lentils (not red)
1 bay leaf
1 clove garlic finely chopped
1 pinch of ground cloves
1 pinch of nutmeg
1 pinch of salt
3 tablespoons olive oil
3 tablespoons apple juice
3 tablespoons cider vinegar
3 tablespoon honey

Directions:

In camp:
In a medium saucepan dissolve vegetable stock powder, set aside.
Bring to a boil. Add lentils, salt, bay leaf. Simmer for 20 minutes. Add remaining ingredients, stirring occasionally. Cook 5 minutes longer, or until lentils are tender.

Thai Noodle Salad

Makes 3- 4 servings

Ingredients:
8 oz. Ramen noodles
1 red bell pepper, julienned
¼ cup soy sauce
¼ cup sugar
1 cup carrots, julienned
½ cup lime juice
½ cup dry-roasted peanuts
1 inch ginger, sliced
1 – 2 chili peppers, (to taste)
½ cup cilantro leaves, chopped

Directions:

At home:
In a large pot, bring water to a boil and add noodles, carrots and red pepper. Remove from heat and let stand for about 10 minutes or until noodles are tender. Drain and transfer to a bowl, allowing to cool. In a small bowl, mix together lime juice, soy sauce and sugar. Whisk mixture until sugar dissolves.
In a blender or food processor place chili peppers, peanuts, ginger, and cilantro and pulse until finely chopped. Add this mixture to the noodles and blend. Then add soy sauce mixture and toss to blend.

In camp:
Serve salad as an excellent side dish to just about anything you are making for dinner.

Slammin' Yammin' Quesadillas

Makes 4 servings

Ingredients:
1 ½ cups onion, minced
1 cloves garlic, minced
1 tablespoon olive oil
2 teaspoons dried oregano
1 ½ teaspoons dried basil
1 ½ teaspoons chili powder
1 ½ teaspoons curry powder
2 cups cooked and mashed yams
4 whole-wheat tortillas
1 cup finely grated sharp cheddar cheese

Directions:

At home:
Peel and chop yams into small pieces then steam until tender, mash and pack in a Ziploc bag. Grate cheese and bag. Combine all dried ingredients in a separate bag as well.

In camp:
Sauté onion and garlic in olive oil in saucepan or fry pan until translucent. Add oregano, basil, chili powder, and curry powder and cook about a minute longer. Add mashed yams and stir well to combine and heat through.
Lay out tortillas on a flat surface or plate. Spread ½ cup filling on each tortilla. Sprinkle on the cheese and fold over, pressing tightly so filling reaches the edges. In a fry pan cook tortillas until lightly browned on each side and cheese is melted. Serve with salsa and sour cream.

The Hungry Kayaker

tea:

In the morning, I need a cup of coffee to get myself up and going for the day but by evening, once all the paddling and camp chores are completed I do enjoy boiling up a pot of hot water on the camp stove and brewing up some tea. You can bring along store-bought bags but sometimes it is nice to make a brew from scratch. After all, you have all the time in the world in camp to fiddle with a few ingredients and in the end, you'll have a grand cuppa!

Chamomile Chai

Ingredients:
3 teaspoons fresh ginger, grated
1 teaspoon coriander seeds
1/8 teaspoon cinnamon
1/8 teaspoon cardamom
1/16 teaspoon allspice
2 teaspoons chamomile, or 2 chamomile tea bags

Directions:

In camp:
Combine all ingredients except chamomile in water and simmer for 20 minutes. Remove from heat and add chamomile. Steep for another 10 minutes. Strain out herbs and serve hot.

Chocolate Minty Tea

Ingredients:
2 mint tea bags
2 cups milk
2 tablespoons hot chocolate mix

Directions:

In camp:
In a saucepan heat milk with tea bags until almost boiling. Steep for a couple of minutes and strain out the tea bags. Pour out 2 mugs of milk, then stir in a tablespoon of chocolate to each mug.

Cranberry-Ginger Tea

Ingredients:

2 tea bags
2 cups hot water
½ cup ginger, fresh and thinly sliced
½ cup cranberries
½ cup cranberry juice
Pinch of nutmeg

Directions:

In camp:
Steep tea, ginger and cranberries in hot water for 15 minutes. Strain and add nutmeg and cranberry juice. Serve warm.

London Fog

Ingredients:
2 Earl Grey tea bags, or Chai tea bags for a New Dalai fog
2 cups milk
Dash of Vanilla

Directions:

In camp:
In a saucepan, heat milk and tea bags until almost boiling. Allow to steep for a few minutes then strain out tea bags. Add a dash of vanilla and then pour into 2 mugs.

Tookool Green Tea

Ingredients:
2 oz. white rum
1 tablespoon honey
5 sprigs of mint
2 tablespoons sugar
6 oz. hot green tea (one tea bag will do)

Directions:

In camp:
Brew up green tea then combine all ingredients into a mug and serve hot. If you want to strain out the mint leaves you can, just let the tea steep in the mug for 2 – 3 minutes before removing the mint sprigs.

Vanilla Chai

Ingredients:
4 cups water
3 allspice, whole
5 cloves, whole
1 cinnamon stick
1/3 cup honey
1 tablespoon loose black tea leaves

Directions:

In camp:
In a saucepan, heat water along with all the spices. Bring to a simmer and let steep for 5 minutes. Add tealeaves and continue to steep for another 5 minutes. Strain out tea, and stir in honey. Serve hot.

at the end of the day:

At the end of the day as the sun is splashing into the sea, or tucking itself in to bed behind the hills it is now time to eat. Unfortunately, you have misplaced your camping spot for the night. Was it that cove you kayaked by an hour and a half before. You stare at your chart, now what? Paddle on into the dusky darkness to some awful crack in the forest lined with ankle-breaking rocks covered in sea slime.

It has been a long day. It started at 6 am with the last minute packing of essentials from the refrigerator and an extra pair of dry undies. Then a long drive and perhaps there was a ferry crossing to boot. Arriving at your launch site it took far longer to organize yourself and your group into the water after packing and repacking the kayak's hatches to over-flowing for a weekender on the wet west coast. Turning from the sheltered inlet into the main arm of water leading to the Pacific the forecast for light to variable winds is in fact, a slight gale. The inlet is bright green and choppy waves are white-capped, as that wind has brushed the hair of the cat the wrong way.

You and your group managed a few kilometers of paddling before it is time to stop for a break. Finding only a small nook in the lee of the winds, you shake off the beginnings of the day and prepare for the paddling portion of the travel day. Outside of your cozy notch in the shoreline you watch the inlet ripple and toss and in the back of your mind wonder, what the hell and I doing this for again? Back into the boats and the bow braces against the hammering winds. You turn into them and they splash hard up your deck. After an hour of this you cross to the opposite side of the waterway to cut a corner into the next inlet and a full view of open ocean at last.

The sun drops and with it the intensity of the breeze. The water softens and the wind waves flatten giving the surface of the sea an oil slick appearance of dark rippling liquid mercury. This is the best paddle of your life you think. Now that the hard work of beating into the wind for what seemed endless hours has passed, life looks brighter. You muster on, exchanging chats with your paddling mates and rafting up to share some salted cashews and marvel at where you are. A sense of superiority washes over you and your paddling gang. You all think homeward to the people you left behind, and how all of them are just coming home from work, as it is a Friday evening.

That luxury of time begins to wane. The full weight of the day lands on your shoulders and makes it just a little harder to lift the paddle on each stroke. The island, Rosa Island at the head of the Nuchatlitz Group of islands at the tip of Nootka Island is now in sight. A mere dark mound of land against the long line of the horizon beyond, how far now, not that far, but far enough. The sun has now set completely and the twilight hours make you feel rushed to get ashore, get camp set up and a meal on the go. What time is it? Looking down at your watch to see it is nearly 9pm, long day.

Closer still to Rosa and the fellow paddlers fall into private time. The group spreads out across the inlet on the diagonal crossing to Rosa. A laugh and a wild splashing ring out far to the right. It is my paddling companion Pete, pretending at the end of the day that he has completely forgotten how to use the paddle. As he smacks the paddle blade on the water and splashes we remind him that shenanigans such as those broke his last paddle in half. He calms down and we continue across. The silhouette of a paddler ahead, faint outlines of three more to the flanks and in ten minutes more we land on the sand of Rosa Island in near darkness.

It takes no time at all to arrange our campsite. Tents go up in unison; we become robotic in our well-practiced movements. As I drive the last peg into the ground, my stove is brewing water to a boil and a brown plastic bag containing prepared curry waits. This is what I call dinner, a fine one. Palak Paneer, an Indian dish of spinach in paneer cheese and curry sauce. I like it on rice which I had already cooked as I started erecting my tent (camping is multi-tasking). I cracked open a can of beer, a sound that screams civilization to me. Comforts. As I squeeze my hot bagged contents over rice and stir it together with a fork thinking myself to be a gourmet chef on our first night out it is then that something savory wafts over the crisp night air in my direction.

A few feet away stands my friend Mike. Steam from a wok highlighted by the glow of his headlamp, he is opening his first aid kit bag. Inside that pouch, a rack of spices in small containers. We all watched on, in some awe as he sprinkles a little of this and a pinch of that over cubes of chicken simmering in a savory sauce. His reward was a fine dinner that took the same time to make as my boiled bag goop.

The object lesson of this trip to was two-fold. One, it is not the gear you bring, what it is made from or how much you spent purchasing it. None of that matter without the people you bring with you to share the hardships and joys of sea kayaking. The second lesson is that we must reward ourselves at the ending of a paddling day with something filling, tasty and satisfying. If you can cook a decent meal at home then there is no reason in the world why you cannot do the same out in the wilds. Especially on a short weekend trip. The kayak is a natural refrigerator and perishables are a lesser concern due to the shorter time. You can pack fresh vegetables and ingredients that would otherwise take too much room in the kayak for the consideration on a longer trip.

You in your kayak have done something incredible. You have gone somewhere spectacular under your own steam, in a relatively harmless low-impact manner. Reward yourself with fine food, which will only be enhanced by the fresh air and good company. Experiment with what works and what does not. I hope what I have offered is of some help in that experimentation in your own chasing away of the Hungry Kayaker blues.

Bon Appetite and happy paddles!

About the Author

David Barnes is a sea kayaker and writer who is not a chef nor has he gone to any fancy cooking schools, he just enjoys cooking easy meals in the great outdoors.

To his credit is a book called, Dreaming in Nuchatlitz. A non-fictional account of kayaking Vancouver Island's rugged places. He also contributes to Adventure Kayak Magazine.

David currently lives on Salt Spring Island, British Columbia with his partner, three oddball cats, chickens, and a yard filled with kayaks.